Best Answers to the 201 Most Frequently Asked Interview Questions

Best Answers to the 201 Most Frequently Asked Interview Questions

Second Edition

Matthew J. DeLuca
Nanette F. DeLuca

McGraw Hill

New York Chicago San Francisco Lisbon London Madrid Mexico City
Milan New Delhi San Juan Seoul Singapore Sydney Toronto

10   QFR   21 20 19

ISBN 978-0-07-174145-3
MHID   0-07-174145-3

This publication is designed to provide accurate and authoritative information in regard to the subject matter covered. It is sold with the understanding that neither the author nor the publisher is engaged in rendering legal, accounting, futures/securities trading, or other professional service. If legal advice or other expert assistance is required, the services of a competent professional person should be sought.

—From a Declaration of Principles jointly adopted by a Committee of the American Bar Association and a Committee of Publishers

McGraw-Hill books are available at special quantity discounts to use as premiums and sales promotions or for use in corporate training programs. To contact a representative, please e-mail us at bulksales@mcgraw-hill.com.

This book is printed on acid-free paper.

CONTENTS

PREFACE

When we agreed to do the first *Best Answers* book, at the suggestion of Philip Ruppel, we were delighted at the opportunity to commit to collecting our experiences and practices in job search from a variety of vantage points in one volume and sharing them with our readers, in the hope that this would make their job search efforts more effective, productive, and enjoyable.

Even though just 13 years have passed since then, the job search process has in some ways changed profoundly and in others has remained eerily the same. In the first book, the Web was only a peripheral way to learn of job opportunities. Now the Internet, with its ever multiplying job boards and even social network Web sites, has become the most used alternative, although referrals still remain far and away the most effective recruiting source.

Many people feel that human resources (HR) folks are still to be avoided—the more popular concept continues to be that seeking out the hiring manager is a more effective way to penetrate the organization and get that interview. We disagree with that view, and hold that now more than ever, the HR point person should serve as an effective go-between and advocate for your candidacy. At the same time, the recruiting function has often been given to an outside organization in an outsourcing arrangement—an approach that can be extremely effective, as long as hiring managers inside the organization are finding the talent they need and as long as the hiring decision continues to be theirs.

When we wrote the first *Best Answers* book, we suggested that résumés sent to organizations were fast becoming the junk mail of the 1990s. That comment is even more valid today, with job search candidates being more liberal than ever about answering job postings and rushing off a reply, since the personal computer and electronic communication channels make it so easy to do so.

We still see some HR folks who think that posting jobs on the Internet and then waiting to pull résumés off it is a total recruiting effort. Only if it were so easy! Job seekers should keep this in mind and continue to give some attention to the Internet when they are trying to land that next job. However, personal and professional contacts continue to be the best bet for anyone who is looking for a job. Keeping in touch and renewing ties through social networks (Facebook, MySpace, and LinkedIn) can be another tool in your portfolio.

This book is intended to be used to enhance your job search efforts, either as a stand-alone product or in combination with our other job search books, including our favorite and most comprehensive, *How to Find a Job in 90 Days or Less*, also published by McGraw-Hill. The emphasis of the book you are holding is on the dynamics of the interview—an essential component of any job search effort. *How to Find a Job in 90 Days or Less* takes a broader approach and emphasizes the steps required to launch a successful job-hunting campaign and take it to a successful conclusion. We have been providing content and answering interview-based questions on job-interview.net, a site with many resources available.

The approach of all our books is practical and hands-on. You should do more than just read the book. *Use it* by practicing its suggestions—do what it asks you to do with a friend, family member, or colleague. Practice answering the questions that are peppered throughout the book, not so that you can memorize the answers and recite them by rote, but rather so that you listen to yourself and, in the process, determine what works for you and what doesn't. The result will be that, when you go to the interview and are asked these questions or others like them, you will be totally prepared and effective. To help you prepare for the interview, you can also find the online versions of select worksheets available on our Web site at mrgnyc.com.

What if you need a quick start to the whole process? Perhaps the interview is in the morning, and this is the first time you have had to look for a job in years. If time is of the essence, look for questions with a star (*) next to them. These questions, we feel, are the most likely to be asked, and focusing on them will help you to be the most prepared in the shortest amount of time—regardless of what questions are actually asked during the interview.

Finally, as challenging and important as the job search process continues to be, we feel more than ever that working, as well as the job search, should be an exciting, rewarding, and enjoyable endeavor, and hopefully, you do as well. Where else do you get to meet so many people you would not otherwise meet and learn so much that you did not know about the people and organizations where you might spend more time annually than on any other endeavor, including sleep?

ACKNOWLEDGMENTS

Any book requires the support and assistance of a variety of individuals who, in combination, lead to the completion of the project. At the top of our list are Matt's colleagues at Baruch College of the City University of New York and Polytechnic Institute of New York University. Among these, we want to mention Al Booke, Hal Kaufman, Abe Tawil, Corey Hwong, John Lynch, Bernie Iatauro, John Miscione, David Falk, and Linda Moore, who have provided Matt with a great educational setting in which to grow professionally and an ongoing forum in which to develop new approaches to a variety of human resources issues. We also wish to thank our extremely talented human resources expert and friend Palma Braks.

Also to be mentioned is Dorrette Norris, a terrific HR professional, and also Andy Gold and Jonathan Opas, both seasoned professionals who seem to know everyone in health care who is in the human resources profession throughout the New York metropolitan area. Each of them has been great to work with, and all of them have helped Matt to gain additional insight into many job searches from a recruiter's perspective in a most challenging environment.

Last, let us thank the people at McGraw-Hill for all their interest and attention. At the top of the list is Philip Ruppel, who has been with us from the start. He has guided us through the writing portion of our professional careers for many years. Thanks also to our editor, Emily Carleton, for taking us through the steps from book revision concept and proposal, to Maureen B. Dennehy for taking it to its successful conclusion, and to Alice Manning, our freelance copy editor, for reviewing with painstaking detail the final version of the text.

LIST OF QUESTIONS

1. *2.1 What were your positions, rates of pay, dates of employment, and name and title of supervisors for the past ___ year(s)?

2. 2.2 How many people worked in your department? How many people did you supervise?

3. 2.3 How did you get your last job?

4. 2.4 How did you hear about this position?

5. *2.5 Were you ever fired? Describe the circumstances.

6. *2.6 I can understand that your position was eliminated because of cutbacks; however, if the company recovers and begins rehiring, would you go back?

7. *2.7 Have you ever been asked to resign?

8. *2.8 What is the reason you left/are planning to leave _____ organization?

9. 2.9 Have you ever been denied a salary increase?

10. 2.10 Were you ever asked to take a pay cut? Describe the circumstances.

11. 2.11 Have you received any other job offers? What other organizations or positions are you considering?

12. *2.12 What is your current salary?

13. *2.13 Can we contact your references and your present/former employers?

14. 4.1 What a beautiful/miserable/cold/hot/rainy/windy day it is, isn't it?

15. 4.2 Did you have a hard time finding the building/our office? Did your plane come in on time? How is your hotel?

16. 4.3 What about those Rangers? The City Council election? The paving of the Interstate?

17. 4.4 I saw on your résumé that you enjoy ___. How did you get interested in this?

18. **4.5** I see that you also went to __ [school]. How is Professor ___ these days? I see you went to ___. I went there myself. Do they still __?

19. **4.6** How do you like living in ___?

20. **4.7** I see that you are reading __ [book/magazine/paper]. Did you see the article on _____? What did you think of it?

21. **4.8** I see that you drive a ___. How do you like it?

22. **4.9** Our team has won the industry cup for three years in a row. Do you play ___?

23. **4.10** What do you prefer to be called?

24. **4.11** What do you think about _____ (any controversial "in the news" topic)? Do you think the economy is getting better? How do you feel about the bailouts (or any other recession-related question)?

25. **4.12** Would you like something to drink? A cigarette?

26. **5.1** Tell me about yourself.

27. ***5.2** Why did you choose this time to leave your current/past position?

28. **5.3** Had you thought of leaving your current/past position before? If so, what held you there?

29. **5.4** Are you looking for a permanent or a temporary job?

30. **5.5** How do you feel about looking for another job?

31. **5.6** I see that you worked for _____ for _____ years; how does it feel to be back in the job market? How did you prepare yourself for this job search?

32. ***5.7** What has been the extent of your job search so far? How long have you been looking?

33. **5.8** What career options do you feel that you have at this moment? What have you done to explore them?

34. **5.9** What are you looking for in a job? What would be your ideal job? Your ideal employer? Your ideal career?

35. **5.10** Describe a major goal that you have recently set for yourself. What are you doing to attain it?

36. **5.11** Describe the best boss/supervisor that you ever had. Describe the worst. What was the best job that you ever had? The worst?

37. ***5.12** How do you feel about your career progress to date? If your prior employer had not had to do massive layoffs, what do you think your career progress there would have been?

38. **5.13** How do you define success? Has your definition changed as a result of recent economic events?

39. **5.14** Which of your personal characteristics do you think will be needed to be a success in this position.

40. **5.15** What would you hope to accomplish in your first six months if we were to hire you?

41. **5.16** If you could, what would you change about this position?

42. ***5.17** What do you like the most about this position? What do you like the least about this position?

43. **5.18** Do you prefer delegation or hands-on control? What is your management style?

44. **5.19** What kind of people do you like to work with? What do you feel is the easiest type of person to deal with? The most difficult?

45. **5.20** What is your prime short-term personal goal?

46. ***5.21** What are your strong points? What are your weak points?

47. **5.22** What is your greatest accomplishment? List your five most significant accomplishments.

48. **5.23** If we spoke to your current/former boss, what would he or she say are your greatest strengths/your greatest weaknesses?

49. **5.24** What features did you like the least/the most about your current/last position?

50. **5.25** What will you do if this position is not offered to you?

51. **5.26** Where do you hope to be professionally in five years?

52. **5.27** Would you consider volunteering or interning at our organization?

53. **5.28** Do you think you are creative? Do others think you are creative?

54. ***5.29** How would you describe your own personality?

55. ***5.30** May I have your business card?

56. **6.1** If you could start your career over again, what would you do differently?

57. ***6.2** What do you know about the position for which you are applying?

58. ***6.3** What do you know about our company?

59. ***6.4** What is the most recent skill that you learned? What was the newest thing that you learned how to do? Where and when did you learn it?

60. **6.5** Why did you choose to learn that? Why did you seek to acquire that skill?

61. **6.6** How do you learn? What is your learning style (hands-on, research, or by example)?

62. ***6.7** How do you keep informed professionally?

63. **6.8** What professional organizations do you belong to? [Or, if an organization was mentioned on your résumé: Are you very active with _____ (group)]?

64. ***6.9** What have you learned from the jobs that you have held?

65. **6.10** Do you think that you have top management potential?

66. **6.11** Why did you go to law school/business school/college? Why did you attend that particular school/college?

67. **6.12** What was/is your best subject? Your favorite subject? Your most influential teacher? Your GPA?

68. **6.13** What made you choose to become a lawyer/chef/secretary/ engineer?

69. ***6.14** What is our business? What do you know about our organization?

70. **6.15** Do you use our products/services? Are you familiar with our current advertising campaign/TV or print ads? Have you visited our Web site? Do you get our newsletters?

71. ***6.16** What do you think our business's biggest problem is? What do you feel is our biggest advantage over our competition?

72. ***6.17** What important trends do you see in our industry?

73. ***7.1** Describe your current/last work group. What is/What was it like working with your current/last work group?

74. **7.2** Let me describe the work group you would be joining if we offered you the position. How would you fit in? In this position, how would you see your role as team member/builder?

75. **7.3** What would be your ideal work group? Size and type?

76. ***7.4** How would you define a conducive work environment?

77. **7.5** What do you feel would be a difficult work environment? Have you ever had to deal with a difficult work environment? What happened?

78. **7.6** Have you ever had to fire someone? Describe the circumstances and how you handled the situation.

79. **7.7** Have you ever had to hire someone? For what types of positions/salary levels? What do you look for when you hire someone?

80. **7.8** What interview questions did you ask that persuaded you to hire or not? How did your hire(s) work out?

81. **7.9** Have you ever had to motivate or build team spirit among coworkers? Describe why this happened.

82. ***7.10** Have you ever worked for, or with, a difficult person?

83. **7.11** How many of your bosses were male? Female? Were most of your coworkers male or female (or in other EEO categories)?

84. **7.12** How much time on your current/last job is/was spent working alone? Which do you prefer—working alone or with a group?

85. **7.13** How often did you meet with your supervisor? For what purpose?

86. **7.14** In your current/past position, how important is/was communication and dealing with others? In your current/past position, what role does/did communication play?

87. **7.15** What form of communication do you prefer? Which do you feel is most effective?

88. **7.16** Do you instant message? Do you Twitter? Do you like to use e-mails? Do you have a BlackBerry or iPhone?

89. *__7.17__ Describe how your last/current job related to the overall goals of your department and organization. What impact did it have on the company's profit or loss?

90. **7.18** Did you bring work home? Did you work from home? Did you take all the vacation/time off that you were entitled to? What is your attitude toward lunch? What about eating at one's desk?

91. *__7.19__ Do/Did you work on major projects in your current/most recent job? Tell me about a project in your current/last job that you really got excited about. What were/are the most important projects that you completed on your last/current job?

92. **7.20** How do you plan and organize for a major long-range project?

93. **7.21** How many projects can you handle at one time?

94. **7.22** What activities did/do you perform in your last/current position, and what was/is the approximate time devoted to these activities?

95. **7.23** What was/is your workload like on your last/current job?

96. *__7.24__ What were/are your most important decisions on your last/current job?

97. **7.25** In what ways has your current/last job prepared you to take on greater responsibility?

98. **7.26** Describe a situation when you had to make a quick "seat of the pants" decision. What choices did you think you had, and what was the outcome?

99. *__7.27__ How were you evaluated on your last/current job? Give an example of a situation when you received constructive feedback.

100. **7.28** Have you been involved in/responsible for performance reviews of others? Describe the process.

101. **7.29** What are some things that you find difficult to do? Why?

102. **7.30** How do you remain effective when you are faced with difficult tasks or with things that you do not like to do?

103. **7.31** How does your current or prior organization compare with us (the organization that you are interviewing with)?

104. **7.32** Have you ever changed the nature of your job? How?

105. **7.33** Have you ever had to make an unpopular decision or announcement? Describe it and tell me how you handled it.

106. ***7.34** In your current/past position, how many levels of management do/did you have to communicate with? On what issues and levels do/did you deal with management?

107. **7.35** In your current/past position, what problems did you identify that had previously been overlooked? What actions did you take or recommend?

108. **7.36** What do you think is the most difficult aspect of being a manager/executive?

109. **7.37** What do you think makes this position different from your last/current position?

110. **7.38** What do you wish you had accomplished at your last/current position that you were unable to accomplish?

111. **7.39** What kinds of decisions are most difficult for you?

112. **7.40** When you have to make a difficult decision, where do you seek guidance?

113. ***7.41** What makes you think that you could handle a position that requires so many diverse talents and persuasive skills?

114. **7.42** What would you do if you had to make a decision without a procedure or precedent to guide you?

115. ***8.1** What is your management style? Provide examples from your current (or most recent) position that demonstrate this style.

116. **8.2** Are you a good manager? Give some examples to demonstrate that.

117. ***8.3** How do/did you interact differently with diverse management levels and types?

118. **8.4** How far do you see yourself rising in our organization?

119. ***8.5** What is your relationship with your former employer?

120. ***8.6** Describe a situation in which the team fell apart. What was your role in the outcome?

121. ***8.7** Describe a situation in which the person you were dealing with enabled you to be more effective.

122. ***8.8** Describe a situation in which you needed to get an understanding of another person's viewpoint before you could get your job done. What problems did you encounter, and how did you handle them?

123. **8.9** How did you feel the last time you joined a new organization and met your new group?

124. **8.10** It seems as if it has been a long time since you changed jobs. How do you feel about joining a new group/new organization?

125. **8.11** If we were to hire you, what do you think would be the first things on your "to do" list on day 1?

126. ***8.12** Tell me about a difficult situation when you pulled the team together.

127. **8.13** When you begin to work with new people, how do you get to understand them? Are you successful in predicting/interpreting their behavior? Give examples.

128. ***8.14** Tell me about a responsibility in your current/last job that you really enjoyed.

129. ***8.15** Give an example of a situation where you had to be assertive/creative/supportive on the job.

130. **8.16** Describe a complex problem that you had to deal with.

131. **8.17** Describe a situation in which you failed to reach a goal.

132. **8.18** Describe circumstances in which you had to work under pressure and deal with deadlines.

133. **8.19** You must have had problems with _____. How did you handle these problems?

134. **8.20** Describe a situation in which you had a personal commitment that conflicted with an emergency business meeting. What did you do?

135. **8.21** How do you establish priorities?

136. ***9.1** What can I do for you? Why did you ask to meet with me?

137. ***9.2** Are you free to travel? Willing to relocate? Able to work weekends or evenings?

138. ***9.3** Do you have any questions? What else can I tell you?

139. **9.4** Don't you think you would be better suited to a different size/type of company?

140. **9.5** How do you think this interview is going?

141. **9.6** This appears to be a career change for you. Why do you think it is a good choice?

142. ***9.7** How long have you been looking for a job?

143. **9.8** How long will it take for you to make a meaningful contribution to our organization?

144. **9.9** How long would you expect to stay with us?

145. ***9.10** How many hours do/did you find it necessary to work each week to get your job done?

146. ***9.11** If our roles were reversed, what questions would you ask?

147. **9.12** Some people feel that spending too much time in any one position shows a lack of initiative. What is your opinion?

148. **9.13** Have you ever had difficulty getting along with others?

149. **9.14** Have others ever had difficulty getting along with you?

150. **9.15** What are some of the things that bother/bothered you about your current/last job?

151.   *9.16 What can I tell you about this organization?

152.   9.17 What can you do for us (that someone else cannot)?

153.   *9.18 What do you know about our organization?

154.   9.19 What is the most difficult part of looking for a job for you?

155.   9.20 What outside interests/activities occupy your time?

156.   9.21 What question could I ask that would really intimidate you?

157.   9.22 What reservations do you have about working here?

158.   9.23 What new insights do you feel you will bring to us from your experience in a different industry/position?

159.   9.24 Where does your boss think you are right now?

160.   9.25 Why are you interested in coming to/working in/relocating to (city/town)?

161.   9.26 Why aren't you earning more at your age?

162.   *9.27 How much would it take to get you? What do you feel the position should pay?

163.   *9.28 Why do you want to work for us? Why do you want to work here?

164.   9.29 Are you surprised to be out looking for a job at your age?

165.   9.30 Your résumé suggests that you may be overqualified/underqualified/too experienced for this position.

166.   9.31 If you were going to Mars, what three things would you take?

167.   10.1 Do you have any plans for vacation this year?

168.   10.2 Do you work overtime?

169.   10.3 How is your health?

170.   10.4 We require people in this position to travel overnight frequently. How do you feel about this requirement?

171.   10.5 Do you know how to use a SuperZippo PC and its major proprietary software package, Bogus Oats?

172. **10.6** Tell me what applications you use Bogus Oats for in your current organization.

173. **10.7** Here at XYZ Corporation, we are a team-based organization. Have you ever worked in a team-based environment?

174. **11.1** Where were you born?

175. **11.2** Are you married? Are you single? Divorced?

176. **11.3** Do you have any children? Do you plan to have children? Who cares for your children while you work?

177. **11.4** What is your maiden name?

178. **11.5** This job requires long hours. Will this be a problem for your spouse and/or your children?

179. **11.6** Where does your spouse work?

180. **11.7** Whom should we notify in case of emergency?

181. **11.8** If you were offered this job and you accepted it, you would be required to work with a mostly male (and/or Hispanic or born-again Christian or any other identifiable group) staff. Would this be a potential problem for you?

182. **11.9** That is an interesting accent. What country are you from? What country are your parents from? You have an unusual last name. Where were you born?

183. **11.10** What do your parents do?

184. **11.11** Do you think you will have a problem working in a department that is predominantly white (or black, or Asian, or another ethnic group)?

185. **11.12** Are you a religious person? What denomination?

186. **11.13** Will you have to take time off for any religious holidays? Can you work late on Fridays? Can you come in on Saturdays or Sundays for special projects? We sometimes work overtime on weekends. Will this be a problem for you?

187. **11.14** I noticed that you did not shake my hand when I offered it. Is there a religious reason why you chose not to do so?

188. **11.15** What organizations do you belong to?

189. **11.16** How old are you? Oh, I did not expect you to be so old/young.

190. **11.17** Can you read well enough to take this test? A more polite version of the same question may be, Are you prepared to take the test today?

191. **11.18** Change drives this organization. How flexible are you? How do you deal with change?

192. **11.19** Don't you think you are a little young to be seeking this position?

193. **11.20** Would you be willing to start at a lower salary level because of your inexperience?

194. **11.21** What kind of discharge did you receive from the military?

195. **11.22** Are you disabled? Are you handicapped? How did you become disabled? How long have you been disabled? How severe is your disability?

196. **11.23** Have you ever filed a workers' compensation claim?

197. **11.24** Have you ever been a target (or victim) of sexual harassment? Have you ever filed a sexual harassment (or any other EEO or human rights) complaint? Have you ever been involved in a sexual harassment claim as a witness?

198. **11.25** Has a sexual harassment complaint ever been filed against you? Have you ever been found guilty of sexual harassment?

199. **11.26** Have you ever been arrested?

200. **11.27** My kids are always sick with colds and flu. How about yours?

201. **11.28** We have a great medical plan. Did you get stuck with a lot of bills last year?

INTRODUCTION

WHAT THIS BOOK CAN DO FOR YOU

You have carefully crafted your résumé. You have spent endless hours researching leads. You have compared notes on job possibilities with family and friends. You have mailed out cover letters and have done your follow-up telephone calls. You have repeated this process over and over again—and now, after all your efforts, you have achieved the long-sought interview! Whether you have just started your job search (by choice or by chance) or you have been looking for some time, you cannot squander this opportunity.

This book prepares you for the most important aspect of the job search: how to answer the toughest job interview questions effectively. Just to be clear: there are no magic answers, no "one size fits all" responses. What we will try to do is to clue you in to the preparation necessary for the different types of interviews and the thought patterns that underlie appropriate and effective answers. It is important that you know that it is not necessarily the best *candidates* that get the job offers, it is the best *interviewees*. The candidate who can handle the recruitment and selection process of the organization that is looking to fill the opening best is the person who will ultimately be chosen.

The key to the whole process is that it needs to begin with you. The very first question you must answer is, "What are you looking for?" Have you recently lost your job and are now panicking about the loss of a paycheck? Are you retired, bored with staying at home, and so looking for a second (or third or more) career? Are you planning to relocate to another area in search of more job opportunities? Have you been passed over for promotion and feel that it is time to move on? Are you looking for a new job, any job, a better job, or just exploring the possibilities? Interviewing is outcome based—you cannot know whether you have "won" the interview unless you know what you are seeking. You might even just wake up one morning and decide that you are ready for a change (when you have that luxury, remember that the best time to look for a job is when you have one). Regardless of your reason, this book will help you to prepare for a job search that begins and ends with you.

With finding a job growing more challenging each day as we all fight for financial survival in this very complicated global economy, this book specifically identifies opportunities for you to shine—not because we provide the "right responses," but rather because of the person-centered approach that asks you for the answers that will show you at your best throughout the interview process. You can maximize those opportunities that position you in the most favorable light, which, in turn, will increase your prospects each and every time.

Our goal is a straightforward one: to identify the most important questions and topics as part of the preparation process, so that when you are called on, you're ready with the best answers—not with memorized responses, but with informed, reasoned replies, drawn from your own background and experiences. What this book does for you is prepare you for the job search process and, most important, for the arduous aspects of interviewing. Remember, a great résumé may get you the interview, but it does not land you the job. It is very possible for a person to get a job without a résumé, but rarely does a person get a job without an effective interview. This is true for most positions in most occupations throughout the for-profit, not-for-profit, and governmental sectors, and it becomes increasingly true the higher up a person moves in the organizational hierarchy, regardless of the company and the industry in which you are seeking your next job.

The skills and preparation that are needed for great interviews are valuable in any employment situation: the ability to communicate, to think clearly and logically (some would add critically and creatively), to be able to assess and evaluate, and to be able to present ideas and sell them to a broad range of individuals.

To achieve the best interview possible, you need to have appropriate and convincing answers to a broad range of questions. To help you, this book is broken down into various categories of questions as follows:

You can see from this list that we cover a lot of areas that are typically touched on in interviews, but you can also see that there is no heading called "Trick Questions." Why? Because what might be tricky for someone else can be easy for you. Stressors can differ from interview to interview and from applicant to applicant; some of us think better on our feet than others. Something like: "How were you evaluated on your last job?" can prove tricky. Is the interviewer referring to the grade you got or the method used to evaluate you? If you are not alert and prepared to ask the interviewer to clarify the question, it could trip you up.

Some interviewers do like to ask "puzzle" or "riddle" questions, and also pseudo-psychological ones (what would they do with your answers?). Questions such as these are not related to the job opening, cannot really be prepared for, and are more in the stress or "What are they thinking?" category:

Why are manhole covers round?

Why does a mirror reverse your image left-right but not up-down?

If you could eliminate one of the 50 United States, which would it be?

Who would you dress up as for Halloween?

Start at the Beginning

How should you start? We said it earlier, but let's say it again: you need to start with you. Build your confidence first with preparation. What are your prime selling points? What do you see as your most valuable assets? Do you have a great story to tell about your recent job or education? Take the time to highlight your recent excellent (and not so excellent) work experiences. (You're not sure you have any? All the more reason to give this matter some time and attention—if you don't think about these experiences, you will sooner or later forget them.) List your most recent excellent experiences first. Next, decide which areas you need the most help on and tackle those. Are you a great manager, but your technical skills are a bit rusty? You haven't had the time or opportunity to take a course in years? Go to education and experience questions first to look for the strong points to stress. If you have been locked up doing research for the past two years, your "personal" area may need attention. This book will encourage you to leave no question to chance. We will even encourage you not to avoid preparing for illegal and small-talk questions. A review of those questions may require more consideration than you had thought necessary and build your confidence in the other broad topic areas.

The goal is to prepare you so that you are sensitive to all the facets of the process and give every question the attention it deserves. While concentrating on answering the interviewers' questions skillfully, you also need to stay alert to the nonverbal aspects of the communication process. Not all questions (or answers!) are verbal . . . and the messages that you send with your entire presentation, from your résumé and cover letter to your choice of attire and demeanor at the interview, should paint a consistent picture of who you are. A big part of the interview process is the messages that *you* get from the organization. You are interviewing not just to land the job, but also to determine whether you are interested in working at the interviewer's firm. Why prolong the interview process if you have negative vibes about the organization?

One last point about all these questions and all this soul searching: you may discover that you lack either skills or experience, or both, in certain areas. Start working on them now, during your job search. Take a class, read books, get out and network with others in your profession, go to the library and do research, or contact professional organizations to find out about meetings and membership. Catch up with your network of contacts that you haven't had time for in quite a while. Most job openings come from referrals. Make things happen for yourself. Get out and interact. Interview others at meetings—people love to talk about themselves. Try out some of the questions that trouble you. Learn from your answers. Look for situations where you can get others to interview you. This is not about memorizing answers—there is no script to follow, but more a line of thinking to be aware of. The more people who know that you are actively searching for a new job, the more chances you have to get lines on future interviews. *Follow the "arm's-length" rule: everyone within arm's length of you should know that you are looking for a job.* You never know who may overhear your conversation while waiting in line at the theater, doing his laundry, or making a copy at the copy shop—and be able to refer you to a job opening. Just keep talking!

Difficulty of Finding a Job in This Market

Today's market is a particularly difficult one in which to obtain employment for a lot of reasons, and having an insight into the organization's viewpoint will help your appreciation of the process. Employers that we talk to are amazed at how frequently job candidates know very little about the organizations they have been invited to visit. One big reason for doing your homework is to determine the health and well-being of the organization you may be joining. There is nothing worse than finally getting a job, only to find out that the firm hiring you is going out of business, discontinuing a major product line that affects your position, or having severe cash flow problems.

TIME

To find the right person (or any person, for that matter), the employer has to make a commitment of time and resources. Given the continuous efforts to reduce staff and conserve cash flow, organizations appear to have fewer and fewer persons to carry out all the tasks required. That is particularly true of professionals in the human resources department, because that is usually the first one identified to reduce headcount.

There are other factors that further complicate the hiring process. When an organization reduces its staff, it frequently includes one or more of the trained and skilled professionals who were responsible for screening candidates. Their knowledge and experience are "downsized" along with them. The price you pay when you are faced with a situation such as this is that you get to deal with over-worked and untrained staff members whom you are dependent on for referral to others in the organization who have also survived.

TRAINING

For the applicant, this becomes frustrating because, even though the openings are there, the organization is relying more and more on inexperienced (i.e., un-trained) recruiters and interviewers who do not know what to look for. The result is that the wrong applicants are invited in and the wrong candidates are then hired.

To compound the problem, downsizing itself—more often than not—ig-nores the human element of the organization. In most organizations, unfortu-nately, there is a major disregard for human capital (most commonly referred to as an expense) and for the organizational knowledge and unique experience of each terminated employee. New interviewers are given scant or no training because people are not highly regarded by many organizations, nor is sufficient attention given to the process of how they are brought into the organization. You may wonder, too, whether internal candidates were considered for the opening that you are interviewing for. It can be part of the organization's mindset to think that any possible outside hire is better than anyone in-house; remember, if you choose to work for this type of organization, that it may well take the same ap-proach to a position that you would like to vie for, looking at external candidates who seem more valuable than any employees whom they have known as long as they worked there.

COST

Whenever there is an opening, there are direct and indirect costs to the organiza-tion in any hiring process.

- *Direct costs* are those that are most visible in the recruiting process. These include fees for placement, costs for ads placed in the papers, travel and entertainment expenses, and fees paid for tests.
- *Indirect costs* are the not-so-visible costs that should be considered as well. The first is the lost opportunity cost that occurs as a result of the vacancy itself and the lost sales that are directly attributable to the lack of staff. Other indirect costs include the time taken by any employee to recruit and interview each applicant, the time to train new people once they are on board, and the business lost while the firm is waiting for a new employee to get up to speed and add value to the organization, or, in the case of an unsuccessful hire, business lost as a result of the new employee's ineffectiveness.

A "Buyer's Market"?

The high rate of unemployment, combined with the continuous reporting of major organizations' latest outsourcing and downsizing efforts, lead hiring employers to believe, *"There are a million applicants out there. It's a buyer's market."* The media are chiefly responsible for this unrealistic perception of a huge surplus of talented people just waiting to be grabbed. The idea is that a low bid in this market is not only cost-effective, but downright astute *("if you don't want the job, there are a lot of others who do")*.

Another contributor to this unrealistic perception comes from the placement of online ads. Talk to anyone who has done it. The superficially aware boast that they posted a job online and garnered a huge number of résumés (400 seems to be the current magic number). But talk to those responsible for sifting through the 400 replies—if they get a single hire out of the process, they consider themselves lucky.

For the real lowdown, talk to human resources professionals anywhere in the United States, and they will share with you a very different view. They will tell you that they feel frustrated, because in spite of the high rate of unemployment, they are having a really difficult time finding good candidates. Additionally, they will immediately agree that, if you post a job or run an ad for any position, you will be deluged with résumés, both electronically and by fax, mail, and phone. *The problem is that résumés have become the junk mail of the twenty-first century.* With the proliferation of the Internet and electronic filing of résumés, it has become easier than ever to generate and distribute a customized résumé (to increase micromarketing effectiveness). As a result, more people reply to more ads or job postings than ever before, but the applicants spend less time determining whether the job opening is potentially a good "fit" for them specifically. And the ease of submitting a résumé electronically encourages even marginally acceptable job seekers to submit a résumé whenever they have even a modicum of interest because "why not?"

WHERE TO FIND THE CANDIDATES

Believe it or not, the most difficult task for employers who want to fill positions is to determine where they are most likely to find suitable candidates. It is easy to boast about the response from a job posting, but the best response is the one that concludes with a new hire. The size of the response is irrelevant. Whether a posting gets 1 or 401 responses, the effort is for naught if none of the people who surface is appropriate for the open position. The truth is that basic job requirements are becoming more demanding, while at the same time, our general population has problems with science, technology, mathematical skills, communication skills, and literacy.

From an Applicant's Viewpoint

Applicants are having a harder time than ever finding appropriate jobs. There are many elements to consider.

WHERE TO LOOK?

The decision on where to apply is difficult, and the competition wherever you do go is heavy. Once the path is taken, the obstacles are huge. The time required to look is increasing because the access has grown. Think about it. In the not too distant past, technology was limited, mobility was less, and sources of information were fewer and harder to access than they are now. The positive side was that you could focus on what was close and important. Your choices were limited, and therefore you had a clearer idea of what options were most relevant to pursue. Friends, relatives, and neighbors all helped to identify opportunities within a narrow band of opportunity.

Now contemplate the current situation. Think needle and haystack. Even when you get a lead and prepare to respond, a variety of challenging obstacles may surface. The most common one is that each traditional advertisement or job posting on the Internet for an opening may elicit hundreds of résumés and letters, putting a burden on the person who is doing the screening, or there could be a software program doing a "key word" screening. If your résumé and letter hit a responsive chord, or if you are able to persuade a contact to get you in the door, you may finally get to speak to someone in the organization.

So Many People, So Little Opportunity

There are many people out there who are searching for a position. Many more people are looking for jobs than there are jobs available. Some say that anyone who wants a job always gets one, and that is probably true in the long run, but all that means is that there are plenty of jobs at the low-wage end, but the number of jobs quickly evaporates as one goes looking up the scale. A look at those 400 résumés received in response to a job posting/ad would show that the qualifications of many of the people replying are not even close to the job requirements.

The Proliferation of Résumés

It is hard to get considered for any job because, once a job is posted or an ad is placed, the organization is flooded with résumés. The problem is getting your résumé noticed and picked from all the others received. *Your résumé must rise to the top on the wave of paper submitted.* It is just not enough to assume that your résumé will sparkle because of your specific relevant experience. It needs to have visibility and be separated from all the others. This presumes a timely arrival, a visually attractive document, a targeted and cogent cover letter, and dependence on the person screening the résumé to be able to identify that particularly relevant experience.

Wild Goose Chases

There seem to be more false starts in the hiring process today than at any other time in recent memory. A *false start* is an all-out effort to hire a person for a specific position (or what seems to be a specific position), only to find that the effort has been aborted for any of a variety of reasons. *"The position has been put on hold." "We are rethinking our strategy . . . reorganizing . . . eliminating the department . . . merging into a group function."* This disheartening news can be presented anytime during the search and even midway through the hire offer. The *Wall Street Journal* carried a front-page story of the public servant from Boston who accepted a job with a major Wall Street firm. The day he was to start the job, after relocating from Boston, he read the *Wall Street Journal* on the way to work and the page one headline disclosed that his unit was about to be shut down. He was forced to go back into the job market.

The Person Interviewing You Is So Young and/or Inexperienced or Biased

The older you get, the younger the interviewer looks. That is not just the comment of an older job applicant. It is often true because in many organizations, there are a variety of misperceptions about the skills required to be an effective interviewer. There continues to be a lack of concern for the training and development of the individuals in the organization who are entrusted with the extremely important task of identifying suitable candidates for the organization.

Where and How to Find the Jobs

If one of the greatest challenges for employers is to find suitable candidates, *the biggest frustration for job seekers is to find the employers who are looking for candidates.* While several organizations are in the process of going through their decision to downsize, the United States continues to have a vibrant and resilient economy. Unfortunately or fortunately, that economy includes organizations that are going through different stages of their life cycles at the same time. While new companies in the newer industries are going through periods of explosive growth, others in more traditional industries are in their maturity stage, and still others are in a period of decline. The not-for-profit and government sectors have their life cycles, too. The point to keep in mind is that this vibrant economy is constantly making jobs available at the same time that jobs are being eliminated. The U.S. Chamber of Commerce is not alone in saying that it does not know how many businesses are in operation at any one point in time, because at the precise moment that some businesses are opening their doors for the first time, others are closing theirs. The Chamber of Commerce estimates that at the present time, there are approximately 13 million businesses operating in the United States. Think of that number for a moment: that is 13 million businesses in the private sector. That number does not include the various agencies of the government and the numerous organizations in the not-for-profit sector.

The challenge for the job seeker is to determine which of those 13 million businesses (or myriads more if one also is willing to consider the other sectors) are the most appropriate.

Where You Are Coming From

Depending on how you got the lead for the interview, your chances of landing the job depend on many different factors. Using recruiters, classified ads, and even the online resources (social networks, electronic bulletin boards, commercial job listing sites, and corporate Web sites' "career" or job openings listed) have both advantages and disadvantages for the applicant (see Table I-1).

Table I.1 Job Search Choices

EMPLOYER'S CHOICES IN CANDIDATE SEARCH	ADVANTAGES TO APPLICANT	DISADVANTAGES TO APPLICANT
Job postings (internal)	Limited pool of applicants	Opening unknown to applicant if not already employed there
Recruiters, agencies	May have job orders and openings	Fees paid by employer; longer time frame; additional screening levels
Job search Web sites (CareerBuilder, Monster, Craigslist)	Large variety of jobs posted	Electronic résumé/applications; large number of potential applicants
Traditional print media advertisements	One-stop source	Too large response; too many candidates at the same time; the right people are no longer reading them
Professional associations	Members of a high-caliber talent pool	Limited to certain groups; unable to control the timely dissemination of information about the vacancy
Schools, alumni associations	Known quality	Limited access; entry-level only
Public (governmental) agencies	No fee; indication of good-faith efforts to adhere to EEO guidelines	Little or no screening of candidates
Radio/TV	Wide reach; limited pool	Without volume, higher cost for TV
Referrals	Get inside track	Friendship may be on the line if the job does not work out
Job Fairs	Can interview with several employers in same day	Can be a cattle call, time-consuming to wait on line, lots of competition.

Our earlier book, *How to Find a Job in 90 Days or Less*, describes a three-step process that commences with a personal assessment. Once that is done, the next step is to determine a marketing plan. The marketing plan considers your knowledge, skills, abilities, experiences, likes, and dislikes, and then puts them aside while you take the time to determine the organizations that will be most appropriate and desirable for you to consider further as opportunities for employment. The last step in the process is to implement an action plan to link your desires and wishes to your skills and abilities. These steps lead you to the interview.

TOP TEN "START-UP" TIPS

1. **Begin by browsing** through the book. Review the questions marked *.
2. **Maintain a daily schedule.** If you are presently unemployed, maintain a schedule that approximates your work schedule when you had a job, including lunch, meetings with peers, and professional groups.
3. **Start working** with those areas in the book where you are the strongest.
4. **Practice.** In casual conversations, ask what others like or dislike about their jobs. See what answers intrigue you.
5. **Take notes.** Write in the book. Do the worksheets. Copies of the worksheets are available on our Web site, mrgnyc.com.
6. **Maintain your friendships and contacts.** Looking for a job is hard work, and you will come across better in your interviews if you are not crushed under the weight of your search.
7. **Get psyched.** Winners focus on their strengths. Do not get stuck criticizing yourself, but examine your behaviors and accentuate the positives. Be realistic in assessing your skills, potential, and experience levels.
8. **Enjoy life.** Enjoy the interview process—meeting people and learning about different organizations. Be balanced: Do something other than search for a job all your waking hours.
9. **Learn from yourself.** Give yourself points for great answers or for surviving a tough interview, whether you were offered the job or not.
10. **Be honest with yourself.** Whether you are doing the math as to how much of a salary you really need to live on or deciding if you are really interested in finally pursuing a change of career, be totally honest. Being out of a job can be traumatic, but it can also provide you with the impetus to make changes in your life.

1

TALKING IS NOT COMMUNICATING

An interview is a conversation with a specific purpose. Both parties to the interview want something from the process. Thus, the ideal outcome of the interview is for both parties to feel that they have achieved their goals. The greater the area of common goals met, the greater the probability of a job offer—or at least a continuation for one more round of the interviewing process.

What are the interviewer's goals? One would hope that his primary goal is to fill the position. However, there are excellent, good, and poor interviewers out there, and *the interviewer's apparent agenda at an interview may differ widely from his real, not-so-obvious agenda.*

- Is this a courtesy interview?
- Has the position been all but filled internally, and the organization is just going through the motions of a search?
- What else is going on politically in the organization?
- What kind of day is the interviewer having?
- What is the interviewer's next appointment?
- Is the interview running late?

Importance of Knowledge Workers Who Are Excellent Communicators

Why should the interview count for so much when the type of skills it calls for do not seem to be the most important requirements for the job? Job seekers are frequently frustrated and feel hampered because they lack confidence in their oral communication ability. Additionally, the person who is trying to find a job may resent the interview process because it represents a real or perceived hurdle that acts as an impediment to job offers. (*"I'm looking for a job, not to have meetings. Why can't they judge me by reviewing my paperwork and giving me a written test?*

The position I seek does not require interviewing skills anyway.")

This is a source of real agitation about the interview process. An applicant may be unable to communicate her work experience effectively even though she may be very successful at her work, and possibly even be an expert in the field. The question may be legitimate: what is the relevance of the interview if oral communication is not a major job requirement?

While many jobs do not require constant interaction with other employees, *communicating effectively at work is becoming increasingly important, regardless of your position*. Technology and change—the hallmarks of our current everyday environment—make it increasingly important that you always be ready to communicate effectively. In fact, the reason that most people are not able to retain their current positions is problems with interpersonal relationships on the job. Failure to communicate effectively can be a real drawback to career progress.

The gurus publishing books on work-related issues today all seem to agree that we are living in a postindustrial age. Only about 10 percent of all workers in the United States are employed by companies in the manufacturing industry. The vast majority work in the service sector, and a smaller and smaller portion are in agriculture. These numbers have not changed significantly in quite a few years. So what is portrayed now as a sudden change has been a reality for a while.

The "knowledge worker," on the other hand, is a concept that is very recent. Even though traditionally employers have usually frowned on the notion of the indispensable worker (their goal was to seek the opposite), there is now a growing realization that *the most desired workers are those who bring their knowledge with them to the job*. What the employer imparts and the employees absorb is a variety of mental concepts that enable an employee to build a personal database in his head that grows increasingly valuable to the employer. In fact, it is being grudgingly accepted that even the assembly-line worker in manufacturing (the most obvious object of the attempt to make every worker truly dispensable) is a knowledge worker. Employers are conceding the importance of the skill base that workers build as they grow with the organization. In the most manual and labor-intensive of jobs, the incumbents performing the jobs are appreciated more than ever. Concern for lost knowledge as members of an aging workforce retire extends beyond manufacturing. In health care, for instance, a very real challenge for the industry is dealing with masses of nurses in their fifties and sixties who are retiring. Organizations are letting these folks go without finding any real opportunities to corral the lifetime of expertise that these clinicians are taking out the door.

If the knowledge worker is becoming increasingly important, how does an employer determine which applicant has the experience (or potential) to be an effective worker in an environment where knowledge is so important? So much of what is perceived to be "job-related knowledge" is intangible, and, even if it could be determined with a written test, many employers would not see this as a practical alternative because of the time and expense required to develop such a test. Thus, the most common and the most practical choice is the "hands-on" personal interview, in which candidates are sized up, their work and education experience are evaluated, and their potential is assessed.

The Interview Process

Invitations to interview are the keys to the job search process. The more opportunities you get to be considered for available openings, the more likely it is that you will have a job search that leads to one or more desirable offers. The more that you interview, the better you get.

In an interview, the first step is to determine that both the interviewer and the interviewee agree on the purpose of the meeting. Is the interviewer looking to fill a specific position? Is this position open? Do you meet the requirements for the position? Given the job description, are you interested in the position as it currently exists?

Most likely, you have already submitted a résumé and cover letter, and perhaps you have filled out a job application. Now you are at the interview, ready to fill in the blanks and "sell" your candidacy. All this should present a consistent picture of who you are as a potential employee.

INTERVIEW BASICS

❑ What is the **purpose** of the interview?
❑ With whom will you be meeting? What is his title?
❑ What information do you want to **give** at the interview?
❑ What information do you want to **get** from the interview?

Hearing versus Listening

Hearing involves your ears, whereas listening also involves your mind. Active listening involves your entire self. In the classroom, you learn how to read, write, and speak, but how much time have you spent learning how to listen? In normal conversations, with no specific agendas, we are too often thinking of the next point we want to make or how we can break into the conversation rather than listening to what is actually being said. How often, when you are introduced to a stranger by a friend, are you so concerned with having *your name* pronounced correctly that you end up walking away from the introduction without knowing the other person's name? That, unfortunately, is human nature. How much more difficult can an interview be when you may feel that so much is on the line?

TOOLS FOR EFFECTIVE LISTENING

- ❑ **Calm down**; leave your emotions at the door.
- ❑ **Be polite** but not subservient in your approach.
- ❑ **Make periodic eye contact** with the speaker, but don't make this a staring contest.
- ❑ **Provide feedback**—nods of agreement, facial expressions that show understanding, body language that is accepting of the message. Be empathetic.
- ❑ **Do not interrupt.**
- ❑ **Ask questions or restate information** to confirm your understanding.

The first step in becoming a better listener—an active listener—is to start right now. In all your conversations—with family and friends, or in "small talk" with strangers—slow down and start listening actively.

PUT YOUR EMOTIONS ON HOLD

Quit worrying about coming up with snappy answers; it is perfectly fine to hesitate a moment to gather your thoughts before you answer a question. These pauses can easily be read as a sign of respect, an acknowledgment of the importance of the question. Take a quiet, calming breath. Make sure you understand the question. Unclench your hands and sit comfortably in the chair; wiggle your toes in your shoes to release the tension, and breathe. Train your focus on the person who is speaking, being careful not to stare. Is she speaking fast or slowly? How much eye contact is there? *Differences in style can create tension, but accepting these differences can help you concentrate, which can lead to better understanding.*

DO NOT LABEL THE SPEAKER

Do not become so impressed by the interviewer as a "provider of jobs" that this becomes a block to effective listening. Listen to everyone without prejudice as the source of the information. What you do with the information can be decided later when you can consider the source and have the opportunity to reflect on what was said during the interview. Do not put up barriers to your listening or assume anything about the interviewer just because he or she is of a certain gender or race or has photos that might instill a feeling that he or she is "just like me." Just as you do not wish to be prejudged, make certain that you do not label.

LISTEN ACTIVELY

Do not be afraid to ask questions to expand on the information being given. Show the speaker that you are listening by offering eye contact. Make slight gestures of affirmation (a smile, nodding the head, comments) to show that your attention is on the speaker. If you do not understand a point, ask that it be explained further or restate it: *"In other words, you are looking for . . . "* For clues on how to achieve this, watch a few news interviews or talk show conversations on TV; the best interviews show both parties engaged.

DO NOT ASSUME ANYTHING

Do not jump to conclusions. Gather all the information available before offering a comment or solution. *Let the interviewer ask the question completely.* Jumping in too early can make a speaker feel that she is doing a poor job of communicating because you just cannot wait to go where she is *not* heading! If you think you may not understand the question correctly, feel free to restate it or ask for clarification.

> *When you asked if I had worked for a newspaper, I said no, I had not, but I had been an unpaid intern while on a work-study program in high school.*

Interview Formats

You need to be aware that there are different types of interviews; both parties should be aware of the purpose of the interview. When they think "interview," most people think of showing up in an office, résumé in hand, for a face-to-face discussion. There are other formats that you should be prepared for, however.

TELEPHONE INTERVIEWS

You sent in your résumé and were hoping for a telephone call to set up an interview. The telephone rings, and it is *the call*, but instead of setting up a meeting, the voice on the other end asks, "Do you have a few minutes to chat now?" This is a "telephone screening interview"—aren't you glad you are prepared? Before setting aside time to meet with you, the organization wants to *qualify you* as a viable candidate. The caller might go into some of the information on your résumé and cover letter, or there could be just a few questions, such as whether you are familiar with a particular computer program or some other technical facet of the open position.

At least your physical appearance will not count with a telephone interview, but your voice, confident or concerned, will tell a lot. If you are totally unprepared, there is no problem in saying something like

You caught me just on my way out, but I really want to have this discussion. Can we pick a mutually convenient time to talk?

or

I am so excited that you called, as I am really interested in the position at _____. I am in the middle of something and I want to give this my full attention; can I call you back in 15 minutes or so?

Now you have bought yourself some time to review your résumé, cover letter, and job opening information.

VIDEOCONFERENCING/WEBCAM INTERVIEW

As an alternative to flying out a candidate, some organizations will do a "screening interview via teleconferencing," where the candidate and the interviewer are conversing over microphones and monitors. It is pretty much like an in-person screening interview, except from a heads-up visual perspective. If you are not comfortable in the setting or with the technology, it can make you go off your game, but these interviews are set up in advance, so you can mentally prepare yourself for the experience.

ONLINE VIRTUAL INTERVIEW

Finding a job opening that you like on a corporate Web site, you click through and fill out the information, attaching your résumé following the company's guidelines (there are a variety of methods used for submitting electronic job applications and résumés.) After you hit "Submit," there is a new screen asking you to complete some follow-up questions, if you please. You want the job, so you click again and are faced with a lengthy questionnaire that for all intents and purposes is an interview, an "online virtual interview." Many of the questions are similar in scope to those asked in an actual interview and are obviously used to screen applicants in or out.

You can be allowed some time to mull over your responses. Take too much time, however, and your "session" may be "timed out."

Types of Interviews

There is more than one kind of interview, and each kind is determined by the purpose of the interview and the agenda of the interviewer.

SCREENING INTERVIEWS

When you are presenting yourself to an agency, a recruiter, or an HR department, you will be subject to a certain number of "screening interviews." The "gatekeepers" doing the interview have basic information regarding the job opening and the requirements for the position. Their function is to pass on only those candidates who appear to fit the position. They will ask direct questions about your experience, education, and expectations and go over your résumé with you. Depending on the experience level of the interviewer, you may be interviewed in depth. But it does not matter that this is a preliminary interview; if you do not pass the gatekeepers, then you are out.

COURTESY INTERVIEWS

You know when you have one of these, a "courtesy interview." You've been handed a lead, called in your markers, and were able to become visible to the organization so that you are considered to determine whether there is anything available for you. You may have been referred by a present employee, a client, a relative, or a neighbor—anyone who has a line to the company and who could get your foot in the door. Be thankful that you are there on this basis, because organizations realize that their best employees are referred to them. Supposedly your lead knows you and the organization, and thinks that it may be a good match. Pursue this line in your interview. This interview may be similar in tone to a screening interview (the interviewer may not know what to do with you), but it can be extremely important in getting a line on a job that may be opening up soon or a referral to another interview. Do not assume the interviewer knows the reason she is meeting with you.

Once you progress past the screening and/or courtesy interview, then you may experience any of the following.

AN IN-DEPTH INTERVIEW

In "in-depth interview," the hiring manager (or human resources or the person who might actually be your supervisor) goes over your résumé with you. Any and all questions are fair game, depending on the type of interviewer you are facing.

Stress Interviews

"Stress interviews" exist. However, unless you are looking to be a spy, the head of a major urban transit system, a school chancellor, or any position that is so inundated with stress that mere mortals need not apply, stress interviews are not common. There are ways to deal with them, as covered in detail in Chapter 9, "How Many Ways Can You Spell *Stress*?"

Situational Interviews

Can you think on your feet? "Situational interviews" involve situational questions, such as "Let's pretend . . ." and "What if . . ." scenarios. The interviewer may either be trying out real-life problems on you to see what you would do or just be in a creative mood. The interviewer is looking for *empathy* and *insight* into how you think: Can you put yourself into another person's place? How would you act? If you have the knowledge and experience on paper, the interviewer can take you on a mini-road test to see how you run with these types of questions. The best way to prepare for these questions is to be an expert on *you*—on what you know, what you have done, and what you want in a job.

After you are done you might want to comment, *"Those were really intriguing questions. Do they relate to real-life situations here at _____?"*

Behavioral Interviews

These differ from situational interviews in one very important aspect: the interviewer is looking for *real-life experiences* that will demonstrate how you have already performed in actual situations. You can readily identify a "behavioral interview" when you are asked, "Describe a situation where you were responsible for delivering services in an emergency." Or the one-two alternative approach: "Did you ever have an employee who was habitually late for work?" It is easy to say yes. Be sure to be ready, though, for the second—and more demanding—question: "So, how did you handle it?"

Team Interviews

In "team interviews," you may be faced with several interviewers at the same time, either with one taking the lead and the others interjecting from time to time, or with you facing a battery of questions from all directions. This could border on a stress interview if the interview goes out of control. Treat each question one at a time, and listen carefully. During these interviews, remember to keep moving your eyes to ensure that you make frequent eye contact with each of the persons on the panel.

An organization that uses this type of interview approach may be signaling its priorities loud and clear. One possibility is that it may have a strong consensus culture. Before you leave, you might inquire as to the reasons for this approach *("Was it me, or does your company do this all the time?")*. It is okay to be inquisitive; just do not ask in a judgmental tone.

Try not to make the setting stressful for you. Feel honored that each of the interviewers was willing to give his time to meet with you. Be flattered that the interviewers are so respectful of your time. Appreciate the fact that you won't have to answer the same questions more than once.

GROUP INTERVIEWS

In a "group interview," you may not be the sole candidate being interviewed. It's not quite a "cattle call," but you are up against your probable competition. A group of candidates may face either a sole interviewer or a team of interviewers for questioning. The retail industry is a frequent user of group interviews.

The Traditional, Face-to-Face Meeting

After all your preparation, letter writing, résumé mailings, and telephone follow-ups, the day of the interview has arrived. Call to confirm the place and the time. Plan your route and your transportation, and allow ample time to arrive a few minutes early for your interview. Some candidates take their preparation so seriously that they will make a dry run visit on the weekend to confirm their route and its potential challenges.

Hi-tech smartphones can be a real boon to the job search process; you can get last-minute weather and news as well as GPS or map assistance in planning your route to the interview.

THE INTERVIEW PROCESS STARTS THE MOMENT YOU ARRIVE

Once you enter the building, be alert and listen to what is going on around you. All your senses should be operating to evaluate this organization as one in which you may choose to spend most of your waking hours for years to come. Consider the overall appearance of the offices and the attitudes of the employees that you encounter.

If you can think of the interview as being similar to a "first date," then you should evaluate the meeting place in terms of the importance the employer places on these meetings. Instead of parents meeting you at the door and giving you the once-over, every employee you come in contact with (particularly in the reception area) could give feedback about you to the decision makers. This is a two-way street: you are also evaluating the organization through the actions and attitudes of the employees you meet.

PREINTERVIEW CHECKLIST

- ❑ The **name and title** of the person you are meeting, with correct spelling and punctuation.
- ❑ The **exact address** and location of the organization, including cross streets, freeway exit, and directions to the office building.
- ❑ **Research notes** regarding the organization and the position for you to review en route (an index card or two should suffice to capture the main points). You should include a copy of the job description/ad/ job posting as well as your cover letter to keep all the details fresh in your mind. Your jottings may include:
  - ❑ **A list of points** that you want to make.
  - ❑ **Any questions** that remain to be answered about the position or the organization.
  - ❑ **Your employment and educational history** in case you are asked to complete an application. (See "Experience Worksheet," pages 101–102.)
- ❑ **Your business card** and a few copies of your most recent **résumé**.

LAST MINUTE DETAILS

- ❑ While you are waiting, **warm up** by engaging in small talk with others in the reception area or on the way to the interview. Don't take it personally if there is no response. Chalk it up to the individual with whom you are trying to exchange a few words; he may have had a bad trip in, may be trying to prepare for a pending meeting, or may just not be a morning person.
- ❑ **Listen** for your name to be called.
- ❑ Keep the **greeting simple**.
- ❑ If a hand is offered, give a **firm (dry) handshake**.
- ❑ **Size up** the interview site. What status does the interviewer appear to have within the organization? What does the environment say about the organization's values?
- ❑ **Check out** the attitudes of any employees you may see. What does their behavior say about the organization's treatment of its employees?

You Meet Your "Date"

While some people may not consider the interviewer's greeting and your response important, they are missing an important part of the meeting. *A person is evaluated after the meeting based on the rapport that is established at the very beginning of the meeting,* in addition to the responses provided throughout the meeting. *Applicants who take seriously every message they send during and throughout any interaction are much more in control of their messages and are more effective throughout the process.*

Since you have taken the time to consider how you present (or sell) yourself, from packaging (your attire and your résumé) to content (the research and analysis that preceded the interview), it is only fair for you to evaluate how the organization presents itself. The interview location is the "sales office." Is the organization, as a prospective employer, making any effort to "sell" itself to you as a prospective employee?

Kinds of Interviewers

Terrific, Prepared Professionals

These are the interviewers for whom you have prepared and with whom you hope to meet. However, as with any group of people that lends itself to statistical analysis, the truly great interviewers are the exception rather than the rule. Meeting one of these individuals is a really memorable experience, regardless of the outcome. You will find that the interview is a challenging but really probing conversation. You will depart feeling that you had an opportunity to provide the interviewer with a complete picture of who you are (as it relates to the position for which you are under consideration). You will take away information about yourself that you either had forgotten or were never aware of. When you are going to any meeting, prepare, be ready, and set your sights on meeting with this individual. Prepared, well-trained, and experienced interviewers are also the most challenging. If they are prepared, they expect you to be prepared as well. If you are not, the interview will not be a very rewarding or pleasant experience for you.

And, Then, All the Others...

When you know that you have prepared yourself and are "on your game," yet the interview seems to go awry, the problem may not be you! If you can recognize some of the stereotypical interviewers that you may face, you may be better able to deal with them.

1. *Well trained, but negative and burned out.* These interviewers have seen better days. You can identify them because they share inappropriate information with the candidate ("I don't know why you or anyone else would want to work here"). They may give a stress interview because they happen to feel that this is what gets them through the day, or they may show disinterest in the applicant's answers. Do not write this interview off. Take advantage of this willingness to share negative information, and consider whether the interviewer is sharing with you reasons for personal dissatisfaction.

2. *Well trained but inexperienced.* This interviewer may be new to the field and may have just completed very good training. This arrangement works if the applicant is not complicated and does not have a variety of information that the interviewer does not know how to process. The applicant should be extra careful to stay within the parameters established by the questions and provide simple, direct answers. A very experienced job applicant must be careful to avoid patronizing this type of interviewer or demonstrating frustration for any reason. Anticipated perceptions of the interviewer might turn out to be at variance with the reality of the situation. If you demonstrate any of these feelings, the interviewer will see it, and you will have diminished the possibility for success and will have very little hope of a job offer.

3. *Incompetent.* This is a terrible situation. This interviewer controls access to the organization, and the applicant is dependent on the interviewer to set up the meetings. The problem is like an "Alice in Wonderland" interview: you don't know what will happen or where the interview is going. The applicant may detect the interviewer's level of training from the questions asked and their sequence. Yet any analysis of the dynamics of the situation indicates that the interviewer either is a poor listener or is going through the motions without really understanding the process (asking redundant questions, or giving strange verbal cues, such as smiling during a discussion about a termination story or a personal tragedy). In this situation, listen carefully to identify any positive signals from the interviewer. Then stay focused on that area of inquiry or interest with simple, direct answers, watching to ensure a high level of support from the interviewer.

4. *Unprepared.* In this situation, the interviewer may very well start with your favorite "Tell me a little about yourself" or "Give me a moment to review your résumé. I haven't had a chance to review it before now, and I didn't want to delay the process." These interviewers become focused and evaluate candidates using all their listening skills. Do not write off this interviewer, but be patient and try to recognize opportunities to "ring the bell" with your responses. If you mention something that strikes a responsive chord with these

interviewers, in all likelihood they will suddenly become very focused and attentive. If the situation really feels out of hand, you may ask, *"Is this still a good time for you?"* or *"Would it be more convenient to reschedule?"* Avoid making a big deal of the interviewer's lack of preparation.

5. *Distracted.* This person seems like a good interviewer, but for some reason your comments are not having any impact. You need to determine the reason for the distraction. In this situation, persistence eventually pays off—or doesn't. Whatever you do, do not take the distractedness personally. Something outside the interview process may have had an impact on the interviewer, something that you are powerless to do anything about. You may seriously consider asking something like, *"Shall I continue?"* You may also consider adding the comment, *"You seem preoccupied. Perhaps we should continue this meeting at a time that's more convenient for you."* And wait for the response. The responses will range from total denial to total agreement. Regardless of the response, a reasonable person appreciates your attention and concern. The outcome is recognition for your sensitivity to another, and that is not taken in a negative way. You can also provide cues to move the interview along the right track by rephrasing questions to call attention to your answer: *"Since you asked about my management experience, I would like to point out that, in addition to being in charge of my unit for the past three years, I have also taught classes in management at ___ University."*

6. *Poorly trained.* This is a tough situation because everyone loses. The organization does not bring back the best candidates for a second meeting, and the candidate is dropped because an interviewer feels that it is easier to say no than to look diligently for reasons to say yes to your candidacy.

TOP 10 RULES FOR EVERY INTERVIEW

1. **Be on time.**
2. **Dress the part.** Look as if you already work there.
3. **Smile occasionally** (not that look from *The Shining*). Aim for an awake, alert, pleasant, open appearance.
4. **Keep it conversational.** Do not sound rehearsed.
5. **Keep your purpose in mind.** What are your main points? What can you do for this organization?
6. **Accentuate the positive.** Put negative aspects in the best light.
7. **Give details.** Quantify. (What was the size of your staff? Expense reductions? Sales increase?)
8. **Do not give monologues.** Ideal answers are from 30 seconds to two minutes. Interviews should be 50-50 conversations.
9. **Ask for the job.** State your desire to work for the organization, and be specific as to why you are a perfect match for the position and the organization.
10. **Follow up.** Right after the interview, send a personal yet professional e-mail message or hard-copy letter thanking the interviewer for her time and consideration. A telephone call after every interview may be an alternative, but something in writing is currently more expected and accepted practice. Go with your gut when deciding whether to send an e-mail or a letter by surface mail. Interviewers have mixed opinions about which is preferred.

SHOULD YOU COMPLETE AN APPLICATION?

The higher up the position, the greater the likelihood that you will *not* be asked to complete an application at this point. What should you do if you are asked to do so? (This is a legitimate question, especially if you are being interviewed for a very-high-level position. Basically, it is your call, but we would suggest that you do it. It is an immediate confirmation of your willingness to cooperate. A way to avoid confrontation when you are told that you need to complete the application, but you have already decided that you are not going to do so, regardless of the job level you are seeking, is to ask if you could take the application with you and come back another day when you have more time for the interview session, since you had not been informed that an application had to be completed before any interview would be conducted.

THE INTERVIEW SITE

Consider what messages the meeting place says about the importance that the organization places on the person you are meeting and the importance that the organization places on the meeting itself.

What floor is the meeting on? What other organizational units are located on the same floor? (Check out the floor directory on the elevator or the one in the lobby.) Then look around the room. Is there a door (for privacy)? Does the room have windows? Does it have a view? The furniture, fixtures, and artwork or other items displayed on the walls set a tone. Does the room have time-sensitive material displayed? For example, suppose it's November and there are still notices for last summer's company picnic, or suppose that the "employee of the month" plaques for several past months are missing. What do these details reveal about the organization and its staff? Do the walls beam with motivational posters? Soak it all up. You need to learn as much as you can about what the organization projects as an image.

THE MEETING ITSELF

If you have received a letter with the interviewer's name and title in confirmation of your interview, be certain to use the person's name—Mr., Mrs., Dr., or Ms. So-and-so. Be sure to pronounce the name correctly. (If you aren't sure how to pronounce it, ask, and then listen very carefully to the response. Repeat the name once right after the interviewer pronounces it.) Don't be too informal and use first names unless you are invited to do so, and be willing to reciprocate. If you do not have this person's name and title (or perhaps you forgot it), ask for a business card or look for a nameplate on the desk or the door. Use the person's name as soon as possible. Doing so helps you to remember it and to establish rapport.

Psychologists say that when we meet another person, we form an impression, either favorable or less so, within 25 seconds. Keep that in mind during your interview, and do not forget that the sword cuts both ways: you are meeting the other person for the first time as well. *"Judge not lest you be judged."* It is to be hoped that both of you separately determine your initial conclusions and then spend the rest of the meeting trying to confirm their accuracy. Do not, under any circumstances, tune out of the meeting because of your first impression. Always be professional and see the interview through to its conclusion. The person you are meeting with will hopefully feel obligated to do the same.

The Concept of Time

Pay careful attention to the organization's use of time before, during, and even after the meeting takes place. These displays, while sometimes subtle, are indicators of the organization's view of time. The use or abuse of time may be conditioned by the nature of the organization's business. Ultimately, the view of time is expressed by the persons with whom you meet, and it is they who set the tone for the organization.

Let me give an example. If 15 minutes or half an hour pass before your scheduled meeting begins, the delay might be an unusual occurrence, or it might reflect the organization's approach to time. What should you do? Is anyone aware of the fact that your appointed time has come and gone? Does the receptionist think that this is no big deal? Is the person you are to meet with even in the building? If you are appalled by the disregard for your presence and that is intolerable to you, then you need to vote with your feet and remove yourself from the premises. No matter how desperate you are, *if tardiness or disregard for time is a deal-breaking item for you, be ready to recognize it when it occurs and deal with it immediately.*

More subtle is what takes place during the meeting. Does the interviewer get interrupted for calls? Was he asked to step out of the room? Was a closed door ignored? Was the door even closed? Try to listen without snooping and see whether the interviewer provides additional data so that you can determine for yourself what is going on organizationally. (Of course, never repeat the information gleaned at any interview.)

Farewell (See You Soon?)

The last part of the interview, after all the small talk and the serious conversation, is the most important part. Where are matters left? Does the organization want more information from you? Do you want to follow up with it? What is the next step? When will it make its decision? Should you be meeting other people? Is another interview to be scheduled? For details on this portion of the progress, see Chapter 13, "Whew! Now What?"

TAKING THE EDGE OFF INTERVIEWS

PREPARE:
- ❏ **Know** your strengths and offset your weaknesses.
- ❏ **Research** the organization.
- ❏ **Relate** your skills to the specific job opening.

INNOVATE:
- ❏ **Look** at your job history and education from a different angle.
- ❏ **Turn** things around. If you were a buyer, could you sell?

FACE YOUR FEARS:
- ❏ What is the **worst that could happen** in the interview? *"I'm too old; they won't hire me."*
- ❏ What is the **worst possible outcome?** *"I'd have to take a lower-paying job in a small company."*
- ❏ What's the **opportunity** for you? *"Think experience, not age. My contacts could boost sales."*

SELL YOURSELF:
- ❏ **Tell** the organization exactly why it should hire you.
- ❏ **Show** the value that you will add to the organization.
- ❏ **Allay the interviewer's fears** (you won't perform, you will take too long to come on stream, you will cause problems, you will be late or absent frequently, or you will not stay).
- ❏ If you want the job, **ask** for it.
- ❏ Right after the meeting, send an e-mail or hard-copy **thank-you letter**.

2

WHO ARE YOU?

WHAT SHOULD *You* DISCLOSE?

As competition continues to pose an increasing challenge to each job ap-plicant, successful applicants are those who are best able to get an edge over everybody else. The people with the best networks, marketing letters, and résumés are able to get a foot in the door. Once they are inside, though, those who are best able to deal with the interview and all its nuances will be more successful in getting a job offer. Listening, nonverbal communication, awareness, and perception are all invaluable elements in the communication process. An-other important element in the communication process is disclosure; it is not just knowing *what to say*, but also knowing *when to share* and *what not to reveal* without being dishonest. (Lying on an application, on a résumé, or in an interview is grounds for dismissal and is a certain way to start a new job totally on the wrong foot, burdened by the fear of discovery.)

This is not a huge task, as almost all interview questions can be reduced to two basic inquiries:

1. Who are you?
2. Why should I hire you (as opposed to someone else)?

What Do I Have to Share with Interviewers?

Disclosure is the sharing of information. It is up to you to decide how much information you wish to share, the extent to which you choose to share it, and how you want to share it. You may disclose something verbally (in written or oral format) or nonverbally (remember the old poker face?). Anytime a question is asked, whatever the setting, in providing the answer, you determine, consciously or unconsciously, how much information you will share with the person raising the question. If you share too much too quickly, others may back away because you are sharing more than they want to hear. ("TMI" . . . too much information!) Share too little or too slowly, and others may feel that you are being unfriendly at best or disingenuous at worst. They may consider withdrawing from the encounter because their attempts at conversation are not being reciprocated at the same level.

Reciprocity

The objective of any conversation (which is what an interview is) is to exchange information at a level that is appropriate and acceptable to both parties. In an interview, just as in social settings, there is an unstated agreement between the two participants that if the applicant supplies sufficient and applicable information, the interviewer reciprocates by letting the recruitment and selection process continue and ultimately by making the job offer.

Interviewing and Dating

Again, think of the recruitment process as a courtship and the interview as a date. Both the interviewer and the job applicant are jockeying for position to determine whether or not the relationship should go further. For example, sharing a variety of facts on a first date may scare the other person away immediately. Or, during a casual discussion between two strangers who are talking on a plane, what is expected is the *gradual sharing* of information on an equivalent basis. One person might say something about where he works, and the other does the same. If one does and the other does not, the informal rules say that there is an inequity, and an ineffective communication exchange results. The ultimate result is seen in behavior (i.e., no chance to get another date with the same person or an additional interview with the same organization).

This is certainly true in the recruitment and selection process. If too much is disclosed too quickly, the person receiving the information is overwhelmed and becomes concerned with what she has just learned. The interviewer is interested in absorbing only as much information as is required for each step in the process. During recruitment, candidates are screened to see if they might be considered, so it is important to give just enough information so that you can proceed to further interviews for the selection phase, where more in-depth questions are asked and topics that are germane to the job and the organization are explored more fully.

You need to calibrate your response levels to your audience so that you disclose neither too much nor too little information at any given point in the interview. For example, going into extensive, elaborate, and technical detail about the intricacies of a position during a screening interview can easily turn off the interviewer; on the other hand, in a subsequent interview, you should expect that the line manager would welcome the discussion of technical proficiency and state-of-the-art knowledge.

If you disclose information before the interviewer needs it, you run the real risk that the interviewer

- *Knows everything about you as an applicant too early* (such as when the interviewer is still in the recruitment phase of the process). Thus, there is no reason to continue the interviewing process (during the selection phase). When this happens, the only thing left for the interviewer to do will be to decide whether to hire or not.
- *Is overwhelmed* and is not happy that so much has been disclosed. Here the real risk is that the applicant shares with the personnel or human resources interviewer information that is best saved for the interview with the line manager.
- *Considers you unable to communicate on the proper levels.*

It is better simply to create the perception that you are astute in the role of a professional and understand the nuances of interviewing, including the principles of disclosure. In other words, don't go too fast too early in the process.

Jargon

The use of technical, "insider" language is a form of disclosure. By using it, you are indicating that you have a certain level of technical knowledge that the other person would not have known if you had chosen not to share it. If you use technical jargon in the right environment, you are considered articulate, astute, and in possession of state-of-the-art knowledge. If you use it in the wrong situation, you will be taken as pompous, pretentious, and a bore. If you want to use jargon, be sure you are current and up-to-date.

Utilize Disclosure Effectively

Job applicants who are sensitive to the principle of disclosure are more effective during the interview process. They are able to better control the flow of the information they are sharing and are more sensitive to being consistent throughout the process.

With regard to illegal questions, even though you should not be asked certain questions, there is nothing to prevent you from offering information if you feel that it will enhance your candidacy (see Chapter 11, "Don't Go There," for more on illegal questions).

Since I have no children and do not plan to have any in the near future, I am totally open to any and all travel plans required of the position, including relocation.

When I visited with relatives in Italy during my college vacations and was employed there for a few years after graduation, I gained a profound and practical insight into the Italian economy that can prove to be invaluable in the travel business.

Disclosure can work for you if you understand that the withholding and dissemination of information gives you an element of control during the interviewing process. *Share information if it can be of assistance to you. Withhold or delay sharing information if it could be considered detrimental. Under no circumstances lie.* Be certain that the information that you give in the interview is consistent with that provided in the résumé, application, and/or cover letter or in prior interviews, and also that it will be corroborated when your references are contacted.

Facts and Figures: Information, Please!

At some point in the interview, basic information will be reviewed and disclosure is not optional, as these are matters of record. Any facts about your educational or work history can be targeted. This information is all subject to verification with prior employers or educational institutions, so be accurate and consistent.

*2.1   What were your positions, rates of pay, dates of employment, and name and title of supervisors for the past ___ year(s)?
The information requested here is data that you should always have available and accessible because every organization will require that you provide it. Usually this is all obtained uniformly through an employment application. Regardless of the job level you are applying for, if you are asked to complete an application, do so. You may try writing in the experience section "see résumé" if you prefer, and the burden is then on the HR staff members to notice what you have done and express their displeasure if they want you to include on the application the data that are already available on the résumé. The fact is that your résumé does not

necessarily provide the same information that is requested in applications. The question is whether the organization's human resources department reviews the completed form while you are there and asks you for additional information. The most obvious details that are missing from most résumés (and this is as it should be, according to the principle of disclosure) are rates of pay and your reasons for leaving other positions.

If you prefer, you may also consider asking if you may complete the application at home. Whatever you do, do not get into an argument with a clerk who may report back to the boss that you refused to complete an employment application. More often than not, your candidacy will end right there.

Be consistent in the details on the application and on the résumé. Particular areas to watch out for are dates and job titles. Be aware of the salary information that you choose to provide on the application because the question may come up during the interview, and you must provide a consistent answer. Otherwise, you are opening yourself up for additional questions, and your credibility may ultimately be questioned because of a discrepancy.

2.2 How many people worked in your department? How many people did you supervise?

This is simple information that you should be prepared to share.

I supervised one of the three 8-member teams that worked in my department.

2.3 How did you get your last job?

Was it planned or happenstance? Planning to find your last job demonstrates to the interviewer your sense of mission and purpose, and indicates that you are a person who plots a strategy and takes action (a skill that is readily applied in any environment). If you stumbled upon your last job, the answer is just not as strong, regardless of the circumstances.

When I graduated from college, I really thought my best option was for a job in the _____ industry. While interviewing at _____, one of the other applicants mentioned positions at _____. I looked into the company and the industry, became very interested, and pursued some job openings. I have to say, that conversation changed my career path in a very positive way.

You need to prepare a polished answer that presents the situation in the best possible light. *Note:* this question can be directed toward any of your prior jobs.

2.4   How did you hear about this position?

This answer demonstrates the quality of your sources of information. If your neighbor happens to be the chairperson and CEO of the organization you are meeting with (or any other employee, for that matter), do not hesitate to mention that he told you about the opening. As a rule, internal introductions work as effectively as anything that is warmer than a cold sales call. On the other hand, do not portray the referral as something that it isn't. If you have no direct connection to the employee (the connection is through one of your parents, for example), be honest about it. Once the person is mentioned, the interviewer is very likely to pursue the comment to determine the nature of the relationship. It is better to hear it from you now than from the employee later.

Who Are You? Unemployed!

This is an area where disclosure may be the hardest and most uncomfortable when you are out of a job. Given the recent economic turns, many people have been surprised to find themselves in this circumstance. Knowing this may not make it any easier for you to discuss your own situation, but it will certainly be a familiar topic for the interviewer. There are many reasons other than the economy for being out of a job: you can be terminated for a good reason (poor performance, sketchy attendance), a bad reason (as long as it's not an illegal one), or no reason at all.

*2.5   Were you ever fired? Describe the circumstances.

Outside of the current economic conditions, 80 percent of all terminations are the result of work relationship problems, according to an extensive survey of outplaced employee clients by a major outplacement firm. If you were the object of a mutual agreement resignation (and you took the option of resigning), you should think at least twice before responding in the affirmative. On the other hand, if you were truly fired, admit it and end with a comment to the effect that, *"I certainly learned from this experience."*

There are many reasons why a person gets fired, including
- *Poor interpersonal relationships with your boss, your colleagues, your subordinates, or your boss's boss.* As mentioned, displaced employees frequently identify poor interpersonal relations as the primary cause for their termination of employment. If this is the reason you left your job, do not share that fact with the interviewer. Even if you firmly believe that relationships with only one type of person will make you an

effective employee, we would strongly suggest that you not disclose it.

Be mindful of the fact that dismissals are usually complex affairs. Even if you feel that your relationship with your boss was the reason that you were fired, think about what you are about to disclose and consider the ramifications seriously. If you admit that you had a tough time getting along with your boss (who, by the way, may have been the worst boss in the world), that is one thing. If, in addition, you admit to having been fired (as opposed to walking out), then you are admitting to two major facts: failure to "get along" and being fired.

> *I was working for the best boss I ever had, and I really felt good about my job. Then she decided to leave and was replaced by someone who wanted to build his own team. I was swept up in the process and became expendable when a suitable replacement surfaced.*

Many people will acknowledge "office politics" as being a factor in the coming and goings of employees, and this can cover a multitude of situations.

What if you were given the option to resign? Then you can say that you resigned. How much more you wish to share is up to you. But if you sound like a problem employee, you will not get the job.

- *Incompetence.* This is complicated. If you were fired because you could not do the job, how does this sound to the person who is interviewing you? The first question to follow may be, "Why was this not detected during the selection process?" Before you decide to admit to this one, determine whether the job the organization is considering you for is similar (or, worse yet, identical) in responsibility to the one you were just fired from. The only way out is along the lines of, *"The responsibilities of the position were significantly altered between the time I was hired and the time I started."* You must then be prepared to give the circumstances surrounding the situation and briefly describe the events that altered the scope of the position—reasons may include a restructuring, new technology, or the hiring or departure of a player who was key to the position that you were to occupy.
- *Lack of work or job elimination.* This is a common occurrence today and is easily accepted by potential employers. Keep in mind the outplacement survey that concluded that 80 percent of all terminations are the result of work relationship problems. Usually employers feel that they and other

organizations try to save their best employees regardless of the situation—but even though they may want to, they are not always able to. If you lost your job because the position was eliminated, say so. Be careful not to use the word *fired* or *terminated* if you can avoid it. *"Laid off"* and *"given a [severance] package"* are euphemisms that indicate that *the loss of your job was not the result of your performance*, but caused by circumstances beyond your control. A "package" even suggests that you were appreciated enough by the organization to rate one and at the same time presents an aura of an astute negotiator (you!) for being able to obtain one.

- *Illegal reasons, including past workers' compensation claims, discrimination based on prohibited categories, and sexual harassment.* A word of advice: *never, never, never mention to a future employer that you lost your most recent job because you were a victim either of discrimination* (based on sex, race, creed, color, national origin, age, marital status, Vietnam-era veteran, or disability) *or of sexual harassment* (making the granting of unwanted sexual attention a term or condition of your continued employment, or, worse, if you were the person accused of the harassment). If you do disclose any such details, the interviewer may dismiss you as a candidate. At the same time, no one will admit that the reason for losing interest in your candidacy is your candor; to do so would put the interviewer and the organization at risk.

*2.6 I can understand that your position was eliminated because of cutbacks; however, if the company recovers and begins rehiring, would you go back?

You can understand why the interviewer would raise this issue. The organization might feel like a "rebound" date, so it wants to delve into your commitment to this potential new relationship.

> *In the eight years I worked at _____, I learned a lot, and I value my experience there. In all honesty, with my understanding of the market, it may be years before the company can win back market share, and I cannot go backward. I wish everyone there all the success possible, but I am excited to move in a new direction and in a different industry.*

*2.7 Have you ever been asked to resign?

Determine in advance how to handle this question if the answer is affirmative. Admit it to the interviewer, disclosing the circumstances as briefly and objectively as possible. When someone is faced with an ultimatum from an employer, the scar is usually deep and long-lasting (if not permanent). Present an objective spin and demonstrate a firm, confident conviction that you benefited from the experience.

I was asked to resign from XYZ Corporation because there was a major downscaling of activities and I was given the choice of taking a position with less responsibility or leaving. If I had taken the lower-level position, there would have been no guarantee that that job would have any more security. If I had stayed, the severance package might have been less or none at all. So I left. It really worked out well, though, because I quickly found a position at DEF Industries with a 20 percent increase in compensation. As you know, XYZ, on the other hand, went out of existence entirely shortly thereafter, and 200 employees were out of work, with only unemployment benefits at their disposal.

As with any other factual responses, be certain that your version will be corroborated by your former employer(s).

*2.8 What is the reason you left/are planning to leave _____ organization?

Never bad-mouth a former employer. You need to cast yourself as a winner who has always worked for and with winners. Do not whine that your employer would not promote you (or give you an increase, a corner office, or a higher commission schedule). Instead, take a broader view.

Some recent management changes have put the organization on a different path.

Recent developments have caused the organization to reorganize; I thought it was a good time for me to make a move also.

2.9 Have you ever been denied a salary increase?

A "yes" portrays you as a person with a problem, regardless of the situation in the organization. Being denied a salary increase is different from just not getting a salary increase. For an affirmative answer, you need to have at least once in your life gone to your boss and been denied a salary increase when you requested one. This does not include times when one was expected. Remember the times when you might have asked for one and eventually got it. We would not even recommend that you consider a situation that warrants a "yes" answer. *An unqualified negative reply is always the best and the strongest answer.*

2.10 Were you ever asked to take a pay cut? Describe the circumstances.

Although taking a pay cut is different from being denied a pay increase, an explanation is required if you have ever agreed to one. With a pay cut, the circumstances may have required your acceptance for the good of the organization and, given the economic situation, may not have been uncommon. If an equity offer was included (as the airlines have recently been doing), then you are showing yourself to be a person with a reasonable yet long-term view that also expresses faith in (and loyalty to) the organization.

2.11 Have you received any other job offers? What other organizations or positions are you considering?

Employers like job applicants who are being actively sought by other companies. Once you admit that you have other offers pending, however, you need to be careful not to disclose the wrong information. Some employers have disdain and outright scorn for their competitors and others in the marketplace. To admit that you have another offer makes you appear attractive to your interviewer. The more you disclose after that, the more you risk taking the glow off the statement. For example, a major money center commercial bank will look with disdain at an offer from a smaller savings bank. To an investment bank recruiter, it may seem odd for a graduating MBA to consider a position in manufacturing (gasp!) or retailing (even worse!).

*2.12 What is your current salary?

Tread carefully. There are three ways to consider this question.

1. *Did you fill out an application?* If so, the firm already has the information, so be consistent.
2. *Do you know the salary range for the open position (from the posting/ad, recruiter, or insider information)?* Answer with a range, if possible ("Mid-forties before bonuses"). *Negotiate salary when the job is offered, not before.*
3. *You have no idea what the open position pays.* If you come in too low, you may be taken up at a "cheap" price; if you come in too high, you have priced yourself out of the job. Couch your response by giving an accurate amount, and if you feel it is too low, add, *"That is base salary exclusive of perks and benefits that are quite generous and should be considered part of a total compensation package."*

*2.13 Can we contact your references and your present/former employers?
If you are presently employed, you certainly do not want your employer to know about your job search until you have given notice. State, *"I will be pleased to provide references from my current employer if a position is offered. If you wish to contact any of my current or former employers, please let me know before you do so."* It is a mark of professional courtesy for you to notify any of the references that you have provided of the names of the organizations that will be contacting them.

DISCLOSURE HINTS

❑ Interviewing is **between** two parties.

❑ Interviews revolve around a **sharing** of information.

❑ The **progress of the interview** can determine where the interviewer is headed, and you can choose to disclose more (or less).

❑ The old adage **"leave 'em wanting more"** is relevant when interviewing. Also, as in advertising and marketing, you don't have to give every detail of a product to induce a sale—just enough salient points to satisfy the buyers' demands.

❑ Regardless of the circumstances, **never lie** about circumstances, employment records, or personal history. It is a small world, and the facts will come to light eventually (or you will get an ulcer worrying about their doing so).

❑ Interviewers may be dealing with **disclosure issues** too. They may be privy to information that cannot be shared.

3

EXAMINING YOUR CHOICES

WHAT ARE YOU GETTING YOURSELF INTO?

What job are you looking for? And why are you looking now? In this industry? At this particular company? For this specific job? And what exactly are you selling: experience, potential, or knowledge?

Interviews involve a sharing of information. Here are some of the first questions that you should ask yourself—before you start sending out résumés and certainly before you go on any interviews: What exactly do you want from a job? What are your employment-related "must haves," "be nice to haves," and "definitely do not wants"? If those who do not study history are condemned to repeat it, then a wise move when starting a job search is to start by analyzing your work history so that you will be cognizant of exactly what has worked for you in the past and what has not. Much of the time you spend preparing for interviews and going through interviews revolves around self-analysis. So let's get started.

What has precipitated your current job search? Are you looking for a job by choice or because of circumstances beyond your control? How long have you been looking, and how has your search been going? What choices do you think you have? Do you feel that you have exhausted some choices? What further alternatives are you willing to consider? What alternatives have you explored, and to what extent?

There are many factors that shape your job search and can influence your interviews. Whether you are preparing for your first interview (is it your first job interview ever, or has it been years since your last one?) or you are a veteran of 20 to 25 interviews will also have an impact on your interview performance. You may be in the process of reevaluating your expectations or requirements. Regardless of the status of your job search, reaffirming your direction or seeking alternatives that you have not previously considered is a good step to take.

Looking at your current résumé, what did you like about your past jobs? Using the "Job History Worksheet" (see below), list your current and past jobs and what you liked and did not like about each of them. Some of your likes and dislikes may be inherent in the job itself and are probably found in any organization, but others may change with the territory.

JOB HISTORY WORKSHEET

JOB: ORGANIZATION AND DESCRIPTION	LIKES: THE BEST PARTS OF THE JOB	DISLIKES: THE WORST PARTS OF THE JOB

What kinds of organizations have you worked for? Were they large, medium, or small; private, public, not-for-profit, or academic? Do you have a preference based on your experience? Of the approximately 13 million businesses in the United States, many will suit your individual needs. The trick is to recognize what you want in your next job. Do you like working for a big or a small company? Do you prefer a structured or a free-flowing environment? The questionnaire "My Ideal Job" (see below) will help you focus on your preferred choices. Even if you feel that the market is not very strong and that you might not have choices, it is worthwhile to see where you would *ideally* wish to work. This questionnaire also

---

MY IDEAL JOB (Circle Your Preferences)

The organization will be	small / large.
It will be in	a large city / a small town / the suburbs.
It should be within	50 / 100 / more miles of my home.
It will be in the business of	service / products.
The business will be	a start-up / well established.
The business will be	publicly-owned / private / government / not-for-profit.
The organization will be	conservative / avant garde.
My position will require supervising others	a lot / somewhat / not at all.
I would like to work	on a team all the time / with others sometimes / alone most of the time.
I want to be supervised	closely / intermittently / from a distance.
I want to work with the public	all the time / from time to time / seldom.
My job should be	high tech / low tech / no tech.
I prefer to work with	people / things / data.
I prefer to work	on the phone / face-to-face / both.
I prefer to	delegate / do it myself.
My new job should be	the same as my old one / different.
My work pace should be	slow / steady / busy or fast.
I want to be paid	a salary / commissions.
I want to travel	a lot / sometimes / never.
I want to work	in a big office / in a small office / in my own office / at home.
My weekly schedule should be	40 hours+ / 20–30 hours / part time / flexible.
I am available	for overtime / weekends.

---

outlines the different choices that exist, just in case you have not considered all of them. As you progress through your job search and the interview process, you should revisit the parameters of your ideal job frequently to reflect newer choices that you have uncovered or changes in your priorities.

MY NEW JOB MUST HAVE *(Possible Items Listed Below)*

Time off (how much vacation?)	Flexible work arrangements	Electronic devices (cell phone, laptop)
Health insurance (medical, dental, vision, drugs)	Employee discounts	Car, liberal transportation reimbursement
	Child care	
Retirement [pension, 401(k)]	Relocation	Time off for conferences
	Sign-on bonus	In-house training programs
Tuition reimbursement	Short- and long-term incentives	
Paid leave for birth/ adoption of a child	Options	

Deal makers: List those perks or benefits that you must have in any new job offers.

_____

_____

_____

_____

_____

_____

_____

_____

_____

Deal sweeteners: List any perks or benefits that it would be nice to have.

_____

_____

_____

_____

_____

_____

_____

_____

Although salary is extremely important, there are often other benefits that can make or break a job offer. What are your basic requirements? Is on-site child care or flextime a necessity? Which is more important to you, retirement benefits or a dental plan? How important is a liberal tuition refund policy? What other benefits would you add to a wish list? Use the form "My New Job Must Have " (see page 43) to list your requirements. This will be useful when the time comes for you to evaluate all your job offers. This list need not be considered final; it is a working document that you will find yourself referring to from time to time as your knowledge is tempered by your actual recent experiences, which in turn will have you revising your requirements more than once as you consider different elements.

While it is important for you to be an expert in your job and your industry, it is extremely important that you be an expert on *you*. Whether you are designing your résumé or cover letter or preparing for an interview, it comes down to a sales pitch—a targeted sales pitch that can be reduced to "You need _____, and I can provide _____." You are selling yourself as a solution to the organization's problem(s), and that can be effective only if you fully know your product—*you*.

Next, complete the "Personal Worksheet" (see below) to look at the particular collection of attributes that make you unique. You may not have thought of

---

PERSONAL WORKSHEET

What I am like: List all the adjectives that can be used to describe you. Some examples are given, but add your own.

Aggressive	Calm	Cheerful	Collaborative
Cooperative	Creative	Dependable	Efficient
Flexible	Generous	Hardworking	Intense
Laid-Back	Loyal	Methodical	Objective
Patient	Perceptive	Punctual	Sensitive
Team player	Terse	Uninhibited	Vibrant
Witty			

_____	_____	_____	
_____	_____	_____	
_____	_____	_____	
_____	_____	_____	
_____	_____	_____	

What I can do: List all the things that you can accomplish. Some examples are given, but add your own. Do not limit yourself to what you do at work; consider volunteer and other activities outside of your job.

Administer	Advise	Assign	Check
Compute	Coordinate	Delegate	Design
Evaluate	File	Identify	Initiate
Lead	Negotiate	Plan	Problem-solve
Reason	Summarize	Test	Update

_____ _____ _____

_____ _____ _____

_____ _____ _____

_____ _____ _____

_____ _____ _____

What I know: List everything that you know about, either through work, through school, or through outside interests. Some examples are given, but add your own.

Accounting	Art	Bookkeeping	Benefits
Cartoons	Computers	Cooking	Economics
Electronics	Editing	Fashion	Finance
Geography	Graphics	Health care	History
Language	Literature	Music	Mathematics
Programming	Repair	Selling	Writing

_____ _____ _____

_____ _____ _____

_____ _____ _____

_____ _____ _____

_____ _____ _____

What I really like to do: Of all the things that you know and that you can do, list, in order of preference, the top five things that you would like to do in your new job.

1.

2.

3.

4.

5.

some of these qualities as selling points, but they can easily come up in an interview. "How would your last supervisor, coworker, teacher, or colleague describe you?" There are lots of possible "What if . . ." or "Tell me about a time when . . ." questions raised in interviews where you need to identify qualities and attributes, not merely skills and experiences.

Think of all the things that you can do and that you know, and do not limit yourself to on-the-job experiences. This is a great way to identify transferable skills. If you are a great time manager or have a penchant for finding "out of the box" solutions when you serve as a volunteer, there are many positions that value those skills. If you break down your job into all the pertinent elements, you may surprise yourself with all that is actually involved.

The last section of the form asks you to look at what you really like to do. If you really like to program computers, but you are looking for a position as a supervisor, this is time for a reality check. Perhaps supervisor positions pay more, or maybe there is a glut of programmers in the area. But if you love programming because of the detailed hands-on work and creativity, will you also love supervising programmers? Can you "sell" yourself as a supervisor? Compensation and financial needs are legitimate reasons for taking less-than-perfect jobs as long as you are honest with yourself about your motivations. (And don't forget that with overtime, the programmer job may even end up paying more than the supervisor job.)

Now, using the information from all four worksheets, write a description of your targeted job and ideal organization on an index card, as shown in the "Sample 'Ideal Job' Index Card" (see page 47). This is your "wish list" to refer to throughout your job search. Notice that it is written on paper, not carved in stone. Make adjustments as needed. You should also determine what level of compensation you need. You may have additional travel expenses if your job search extends outside your immediate area, or you may no longer be able to carpool to the office. How much money do you need? Then, as you review various job offers and benefit packages, you must evaluate how much each position should pay.

SAMPLE "IDEAL JOB" INDEX CARD

My ideal job will be in a large international corporation headquartered in a city within a 90-minute commute from my home. I would like a high-tech, innovative private company. I can work weekends and travel as needed; I am great working with others in person and on the phone. Love to have own office, but not needed; hate big offices with cubbies. Must have good medical/dental plan; profit sharing a plus. Not interested in retirement benefits now. Position: supervise 10 to 15 programmers, make own dept. hiring decisions and budget; love to design new programs. Salary $85–95,000.

Getting Specific and Doing Your Homework

As stated earlier, it is not necessarily the best candidate who gets the job; it's usually the best interviewee. Make that the *best-informed* interviewee. You need to be an expert on you, but you must also understand your market. Go to the library or the Internet and look for any available information about your target organizations, industries, and/or profession. Just because you have 20 years' experience in the industry does not necessarily mean that you have kept up to date; look into trade magazines, professional associations, and Web sites. Reference books and directories—such as those published by Standard & Poor's, Dun & Bradstreet, Dow Jones (with an online directory), Moody's Investors' Service, and Polk's—as well as periodicals and industry publications, can prove to be of great assistance. Not only are organization Web sites great for gathering company information, but you can check out their job postings as well.

Okay, with All That in Mind, What Are Your Targets?

What companies in what industries are you going to seek to interview with? In the "My Targets" worksheet (see page 48), list five companies that you are targeting at this time. You will update this list regularly; it is good to have a working list of five targets to focus on at all times.

	Industry	Organization	Position
MY TARGETS			
1.			
2.			
3.			
4.			
5.			

What Types of Organizations Are You Targeting or Interviewing With?

You need to research each of your targets so that you can have an intelligent, comprehensive conversation with the interviewer. You also need to have some information to determine whether this is actually an organization that you would want to work for. How does its description match that of your ideal job?

- Is the organization private or publicly traded?
- Is it international or local?
- How long has it been in business?
- What exactly is its business?
- How many employees are on-site?
- Who are its competitors?
- How big is it?
- How has business been lately?
- How does the organization conduct its business?
- What major trends or problems might affect it?
- Where is it in its organizational life cycle?

If appropriate, call up the organization and request a recent annual report or any other publications (an alternative is to get a copy online, but the advantage of calling is to experience what it feels like to have contact with the organization). On-line, use a search engine to search for news articles regarding outside and differing opinions of the organization, its product(s), its industry, and/or its management. Use the "Organization Fact Sheet" (see page 50) to gather facts about the organization. You can create a "file" by attaching any articles or additional information regarding the organization or the industry. Other information to add would be:

- How did you learn of this job opening?
- How long has the job been open?
- What is the job description?
- What about salary and benefits?
- Any contacts? Names/titles/department/e-mail address and/or phone number.

Now, compare the "My Targets" worksheet with the information on your "Ideal Job" and "Organization Fact Sheet." How close are you? Do you have enough information? What additional information do you need? On a "Sample 'Need to Know' Index Card" (see below), list information that you need to gather prior to your interview or questions to ask at the interview itself. As you get additional information, add it to your file or your "Organization Fact Sheet." By the time you go to the interview, you should have gone through several versions of the "Need to Know" index card, with only a few points left to be covered.

SAMPLE "NEED TO KNOW" INDEX CARD

How long has the position been open? (Lots of turnover?)
Does marketing report directly to the president?
  If not, whom does it report to?
Physical offices: rumor that it's cramped for space? Visit?
Finances: Privately held! How is it doing?
Size of department's annual budget/staffing requirements?
  When is the budget done? (Will I get to do it?)
Organization chart: others on "my" level?
How is the department viewed by senior management?
Does the organization like the current ad campaigns, or is it planning to
  outsource in future? What percent is spent annually in various media?

The side benefit of all this research, both in anticipation of the interview and from the interview itself, is that you are learning a lot about the business, the market, the industry, the competition, and current events, all of which can be useful on further interviews or after you are hired.

ORGANIZATION FACT SHEET

Organization Name:
Address:
Telephone:
URL:
Directions:
Contact person:
          Title:
          Telephone number:
          E-mail address:
          Office location:
          Referred by:
          How initial contact made:
Business:
Started in:
Number of employees:
Number of locations/sites:
Ownership:
Senior management:
Recent sales/earning:
Trend for the past five years:
Markets:
Market share:
Leading competitors:
Trends/recent developments:
Other information:
Position: Job title:
          Description:
          Major responsibilities:
          Size of unit:
          Location of unit:
          Salary range:
          Reports to/supervisor:
          Other information:

Experience vs. Potential: Which One Matters?

Which is more important, experience or potential? A recruiter for a major New York City global money center bank remarked that one of the frustrating aspects of the job search process is that, depending on the background and role of the interviewer, either one might matter more than the other. The issue is of such importance because, depending on the interviewer and his organizational position, either experience or potential will be considered so much more important than the other that it will be considered exclusively in every situation. Frequently, personnel/human resources professionals may insist on screening for only those candidates that meet the line manager's job requirements to a "t." Line managers, on the other hand, are usually more liberal in considering candidates. Fit and attractiveness (i.e., the total presentation) may be weighed more heavily than skill level and actual experience. The following comparison gives you some insight into which matters more, depending on who is interviewing you.

WHICH MATTERS MORE?	
Experience	**Potential**
Interviewed by HR	Interviewed by line staff
Looking to match criteria; screening candidates	Looking to fit the position; assumes that criteria match
Concerned about internal credibility	Concerned with solving problems

An interview is an informed conversation that is also a selling opportunity. The interviewer may be trying to "sell" you on the position and the organization, and you are trying to "sell" yourself as the ideal hire! What must the interviewer learn about you from the interview? What information is not contained in your résumé that you want to be sure is discovered?

The interviewer is looking for "can do" (what are your skills, attributes, and experiences?), "will do" (do you have what it takes to work here?), and "fit" (will you add value to the team and the organization?). In order to sell yourself as a solution, you have to convey that you know the organization and the job and that you have insights into the organization's problems and challenges.

Thirteen million businesses! How can you master an understanding of all of those so that you find the job that you really want in the organization that you really want? The fact is, you never will. Get over it, but at the same time admit that the more you reflect on what you are all about and the more time you spend scanning the marketplace, the greater your likelihood of finding the right job in the best organization for you, and the better your chances of finding what you need if you are to be successful. There is no substitute for an ongoing effort in this never-ending process. To pretend otherwise is to sell yourself short.

YOUR JOB CHOICES

Full Time, Part Time, Consultant
Same Job

        Same company
        Different company, same industry
        Different company, different industry

Similar/Related Job

        Same company
        Different company, same industry
        Different company, different industry

Different Job

        Same company
        Different company, same industry
        Different company, different industry

4

"SO GLAD TO MEET YOU"

THE INTERVIEW BEGINS

Small talk is the lubricant of social interaction. It is something to be used (and perfected) in a variety of situations—personal and professional—and it sets the tone for the whole conversation. People who demonstrate a facility for small talk inevitably impress everyone they meet. Even the few who detest small talk may envy the experts' facility with words. This beginning of the interview may be only a few minutes, a few exchanges between both parties, but it needs to be considered integral to the entire process, since it is a major contributor to the tone of the conversation (and the evaluation) that follows.

Face-to-face conversation has been reduced in importance by TV, cell phones, the Internet, and instant messaging. Now, with the proliferation of Twitter, texting, and the myriad social networking sites, posting comments has replaced the give-and-take of conversations. Back in the days before these electronic devices, people had to be *active* participants in the listening process because real-time conversation demanded that the listener concentrate and participate in the process.

With the advent of TV and now online media, receivers of messages can be much more laid-back because the visual image gives viewers three opportunities to "hear" what was said. First, they take in the audio message. Second, they absorb the visual images on the screen. Third, many programs offer closed captions so that the audience can read the message in addition to seeing and hearing it. We can even "pause" the entire conversation and resume it at will! With the proliferation of talk shows, small talk has diminished in value because time is so limited and people's attention spans are reduced. (Remember when TV commercials were one minute long? Now 20 seconds is the norm.) The talk show host dives into the hot topic of the day! In many ways, communication and interaction have been reduced to sound bites.

The Problem with Most Small Talk—You Need an Agenda

The problem with most small talk is that the persons involved are not aware of a basic but essential element of small talk: it must be conducted with a clearly understood, if informal, agenda if it is to be effective.

The most natural agendas for small talk are those that you have in common with others around you: in a supermarket line—the long wait, sale items, high prices, and a favorite cashier. We have all found ourselves in similar circumstances—stuck on a long airplane flight, on a late train, or waiting for a delayed office appointment with the doctor or dentist—when chatting with others (or being chatted to) is one way to pass the time. We have all met people for the first time and sought for ways to make them feel welcome and comfortable. *In the interview process, small talk is one way to break the ice and establish some rapport.* The interviewer hopes that this is one more opportunity to unlock your deepest secrets in his search for the "perfect" hire.

Effective small talk in the interview process, while triggering your active listening mode, achieves two important objectives:

1. It allows the organization to *appear to be "people-oriented"* through personal attention to the candidate and vice versa.
2. It sets a *tone of goodwill and positive feelings* that enhances the interview and encourages the applicant to relax and be more open.

Interviewers have a responsibility to the organization to screen in all the candidates that they feel are serious candidates who meet the three qualifications for the position: having the knowledge, skills, and abilities to do the job ("can do"); having the motivation ("will do"); and, sometimes most important, being considered to be good matches for the organization ("fit"). If the tone is set properly, the organization and its representatives are accomplishing their objective: to learn as much as they can about the person without being exceedingly intrusive. And you, too, as the eager and well-prepared candidate, can learn about the job and the organization and deliver all your sales points—while making the whole process enjoyable for those with whom you meet.

You Arrive for the Interview

Once you are physically on site for your interview, you are more likely to come in contact with people who are assigned to the department you are meeting with. Use this opportunity to "warm up" by getting a feeling for the temperament of the people who work for the organization. Take every opportunity for a verbal exchange. Everyone counts. If someone opens the door, thank her. If security needs to give you access, provide identification when asked. You reach the receptionist's desk. A professional greeting before you state the name of the person you are to meet with sets a nice tone.

These oral exchanges also warm up your listening skills. Icebreakers should trigger your listening skills so that you are set for the real business of the interview. This is particularly important early in the day because you may have spent all your time and effort since rising literally talking to yourself and getting ready for this meeting. The more you make a conscientious attempt to hear and listen to what is going on around you, the more prepared you will be to listen to what is being said when the interview commences.

You can initiate small talk, too. You are not confined to responding to questions. This may be an opportunity to comment on an article in a periodical that you read in the waiting area, whether the subject was organization-related or not. If the person you are meeting with (or the department) is mentioned, certainly give it a try without being obsequious.

While I was waiting today, I saw the article in your newsletter that discussed the major role your department played in the organization's annual blood drive. I can appreciate what it took to take responsibility for that project, because when I was at XYZ Enterprises, I participated in our blood drive for five years in a row.

This gives the interviewer the opportunity to ask a follow-up question (such as, "Oh, did you have to arrange the kick-off dinner as well?") and to search for similarities in approach and challenges.

Even though this portion of the interview is important for the tone it sets, at the same time you need to be careful that it is kept to a very brief time period so that you have sufficient time to devote to your opportunities to sell yourself as someone who will add real value to the organization.

First impressions are hard to overcome; do not come across as unprofessional by carrying on too long about inconsequential topics. You want to appear friendly, open, and excited to get on with the real business of the meeting, so listen for cues to move on to other subjects.

AVOID CONTROVERSIAL TOPICS AT ALL COSTS

If the article that caught your eye addresses a strike (settled or not) at the organization, wait until later to raise the matter (if it needs to be addressed at all). Also watch out for hot topics that are unrelated to the organization. If you have been referred to the organization and have insider information, do not flaunt it. You do not know what the interviewer may know (or not be privy to).

Look around the interviewer's office for topics to talk about. If the office has windows and a nice view, mention it. There may be group photos, trophies, framed pictures, or a golf putting platform—any of these may be fair game for a quick comment. Think before you speak, and make as conservative a statement as possible. *"Is that a basketball trophy?"* presents the question in a way that requires only a simple yes or no, but more likely will generate comments as well. Remember too that the office may have been borrowed for the interview so those personal items you may wish to mention may not even belong to the person you are meeting with.

4.1   What a beautiful/miserable/cold/hot/rainy/windy day it is, isn't it?

This is a giveaway. Don't get into a dialogue worthy only of the Weather Channel. Even in these controversial times, people can still agree that there is nothing that can be done about the weather.

4.2   Did you have a hard time finding the building/our office? Did your plane come in on time? How is your hotel?

Consider your responses to any questions about your arrival very carefully if the organization provided travel arrangements. You want to avoid commenting negatively on anyone's weak performance and shedding an unfavorable light on your own situation. *"Thanks for such easy-to-follow directions." "Air travel is such a challenge these days, but the airport was so convenient to the hotel."* With a comment like this, you accomplish two things: you pretty much close the discussion of the topic extremely quickly, since you are hoping to move on to more important issues (namely, yourself and the job opening), and the tone you set is totally positive. It is a small issue, and you are paying a compliment to those responsible. You cannot lose with this type of response. If the interviewer has had totally terrible experiences with the same group, the worst he can do is indicate that and perhaps express surprise at the results you obtained. But you are not faulted regardless. If you had problems, and if you feel they need to be brought up at all, try to minimize them. You need to put this question behind you in a positive way so that you can get to the real questions, where time needs to be given to your important answers.

However, *if you were late for the interview* (whether because of the firm's poor directions or because of your own errors), keep the problems to yourself. Apologize quickly (this may have been the interviewer's agenda in raising the question) and accept the responsibility for the lateness yourself.

I know I am late. I am terribly sorry. I should have anticipated more of a delay during rush hour. If I have inconvenienced you, let me suggest a new date, and I promise you that I will be on time.

These types of questions may be inserted at the beginning of the interview, and you may lead off by disclosing an item that begs for a response. For example, in response to, "Did you have trouble finding us?" your response may be, *"No, because my chess club frequently meets in the building across the street."* The interviewer then has an opportunity to ask a follow-up question, such as, "Oh, are you a serious chess player?" Inserting this kind of data personally, instead of on your résumé, allows you to be spontaneous and take advantage of any clues in the interviewer's office (a chess set in the far corner of the bookshelf or a photo of her at a chess tournament). An even stronger answer to consider, if true, is, *"Not at all since I did a dry run last week to be certain I knew what it would take to make this appointment."* Here you are stating quite briefly that not only are you taking this meeting very seriously but that you also plan ahead as a matter of practice.

4.3   What about those Rangers? The City Council election? The paving of the Interstate?

Presumably your job search has not precluded your reading newspapers, watching news programs, or scanning Internet news Web sites. If you are traveling to another city, try to read a local paper in advance to determine what is in the news. Besides making you aware of local issues, a local newspaper provides insight into the area, both as a possible place for you to move to and as the arena in which the organization itself plays. *The more you know about how and where the organization operates, the better prepared you are.*

4.4   I saw on your résumé that you enjoy ___. How did you get interested in this?

This question demonstrates two things:

1. You control the data that you wish to share.
2. Once you provide the data on your résumé, it is fair game for a line of inquiry.

Give a brief statement that answers the question. Consider it in advance so that it shows that you don't just jump into things haphazardly. At the same time, phrase the answer to indicate that you are always open to the new and different, but that golf or coin collecting never gets in the way of job performance.

Including this type of information on your résumé may be more trouble than it's worth. Why take the risk of exposing yourself to an argumentative "expert" with a job-irrelevant issue like hobbies or special interests when there is no reason to do so? Second, why lift your apprehension for the meeting because you have to worry whether the person you are dealing with is an expert on the subject or hates your hobby or whether you are perceived as being too caught up in your outside activities to concentrate on the job at hand?

4.5 I see that you also went to __ [school]. How is Professor ___ these days? I see you went to ___. I went there myself. Do they still __?

Share the answer if you know it. If you do not, admit it without apology and perhaps a very brief explanation of why you do not know. *("Since I had a full-time job while I was attending school, I really did not get to meet a lot of students or faculty.")* The interviewer should understand that, even though you and a favorite instructor were at XYZ University at the same time, you may never have taken the instructor's course and may not even recognize her name. Do not go on the defensive. If you pretend that you know someone when you don't, you then will have to worry about the next question. If you keep up with the alumni association or have a family member who is attending the school, briefly share this with the interviewer. Again, you have no idea as to whether the interviewer had a good time at the school or not. So do not enthuse or complain about your alma mater; you may risk landing on the wrong side of the issue.

4.6 How do you like living in ___?

Be positive. Even if you think it is the worst place in the world, try in advance to identify something about it that you can mention in an attractive light. If the place is controversial (e.g., New York City or Detroit) and you wish to hedge your answer, give a balanced opinion such as, *"It's a terrific place because you don't need a car."* By making the statement and being brief, you are showing your interest in addressing the question directly and giving it importance because the interviewer has determined that it is important enough to ask. While you are answering, watch the interviewer for nonverbal clues to determine whether he agrees or disagrees. If he has heard enough, the line of questioning ends there. If he wants to know more and your reply has stirred his interest, he will continue with a follow-up question.

Watch, too, for a sneaky hint of the originator's bias in the communication of the question. This question may be loaded with prejudice. If the location has a reputation for high crime or a high incidence of a social problem (e.g., drugs) or disease (e.g., there is a community on Long Island with a higher-than-normal rate of cancer among its residents), there could be a hidden agenda.

4.7 I see that you are reading __ [book/magazine/paper]. Did you see the article on _____? What did you think of it?

As we mentioned in our discussion of the inclusion of interests and hobbies on your résumé, you control what you share with the interviewer through oral and written communication. However, don't forget that disclosure goes beyond that. Your whole appearance sends a message. That includes anything that you carry with you (a bag, a briefcase, and anything in them that you take out and show to anyone during the process).

If you want to show that you read the *Economist* (and/or the *Wall Street Journal*), bring a copy and read it while you are waiting. The same is true for any other publication or book. Once you choose to use this procedure, however, you are fair game to be tested on your knowledge of the publication. Be wary of publications when you are interviewing in the publishing field; you do not want to advertise the competition's attraction. The same could be true of fashions, fragrance, and jewelry; look at labels or brands that may be obvious.

Think minimalist. Avoid carrying more than is absolutely necessary so that you have the instantaneous ability to obtain what you need whenever you need it. Always have several copies of your résumé, but don't bring a pile of reading material with you. If you want to keep yourself occupied if there should be an extended wait, bring a small magazine or book that you can put inside your bag.

4.8 I see that you drive a ___. How do you like it?

This question indicates two things about interviewers. First, they want to show that they noticed the vehicle you are driving. Second, they want you to know that they recognized it and thought it important enough to ask you a question about it. Whether or not the only purpose for the question is as an opportunity to ask a small talk question to set you at ease, treat it as such, and be brief and to the point.

If it is the worst car you have ever owned, do not let on. Be positive. If the car has a terrible reputation (deserved or not), or if your vehicle is held together mainly by duct tape, consider borrowing someone else's vehicle for the meeting. Some people measure others by the vehicle they drive (or the place they live); the vehicle chosen becomes one more opportunity to judge the choices made by the applicant. If you are applying for a job with an organization in the automobile industry, consider whether your vehicle is regarded as belonging to the competition.

Always assume that you might need to use your vehicle to transport yourself and one or more company representatives to a meeting at a different site. How much would you cringe if the interviewer were to suggest going over to the firm's other site 1/2 mile away, and would you mind driving her over in your car? With that in mind, always ensure that the interior of your car is in pristine shape. Baby seats, coffee cups, and papers strewn about do not usually contribute to a favorable impression. A tidy and spotless interior always does.

4.9 Our team has won the industry cup for three years in a row. Do you play ___?

If your résumé says that you do, the question should be a no-brainer. On the other hand, you may take this as an opportunity to qualify your level of performance. Be realistic and do not apologize. If you are aware of the quality and/ or level of play at this organization, and you feel that you are able to join the team, say so. Organizations that take their sports seriously may choose between you and another candidate who does not play based on that. If you do not play, express an interest in watching a game, if appropriate. Inquire as to where and when the organization plays. Does the interviewer play? If you are sincere, ask if you can attend a game.

> *Funny, a few months ago, when I was crossing Central Park, I happened to see a softball game in progress. Folks on the benches were cheering wildly, and I had to see what was going on; it was your team against _____, and I happened to catch the end of the ninth inning, where you won. I don't play, but I am a fan of the game.*

4.10 What do you prefer to be called?

This is a considerate question that indicates that the interviewer wishes to make you comfortable by addressing you the way you wish to be addressed. With today's diversity, even a common name like Matthew can have three alternatives: Matthew, Matt, and Mattie. Interviewers show their concern by acknowledging that something as direct as a name is not to be taken for granted. If you really prefer one version over others and it is important to you, mention it even if the question is not asked. *Your name is important to you, and you get to determine the impact that it has on the interviewer.* Interviewers who cannot say your name as requested, even after you mention it, may be poor listeners, and therefore your meeting is unfortunately highly suspect. Why not find that out sooner rather than later and adjust your sights accordingly? The other side of the coin is that you should ascertain that you are using the proper form and pronunciation of your interviewer's name.

If your name is that important to you, don't forget to share that information as soon as you can, including taking the opportunity before the meeting. Your correspondence and even your résumé could easily contain the derivative or nickname that you very strongly prefer. If your nickname is a little on the cutesy side (e.g., Bucky, Dee-Dee), consider strongly the image you are projecting and the tone of the organization you are presenting yourself to (shirtsleeves or three-piece suits, Chanel or Betsey Johnson) before sharing this. If you are hired, you can always reveal your alter identity to those you choose.

4.11 What do you think about_____ (any controversial "in the news" topic)? Do you think the economy is getting better? How do you feel about the bailouts (or any other recession-related question)?

Questions of this type that may crop up during the small-talk portion of the interview. This may be a chance for the interviewer to see if you are keeping up with current events, or it may just be friendly banter on a topic that, for whatever reason, the interviewer feels you should know about. Tread carefully—one job candidate recently boasted at a music company interview that she loved Bruce Springfield. After the meeting was over, she realized that she had meant Bruce Springsteen.

This seemingly innocuous line of inquiry may provide an opportunity for the interviewer to probe into your beliefs and political opinions to determine if those views are acceptable to her. Show that you are informed, but try to avoid taking sides, both before and after the interviewer reveals her views of the issue—if she chooses to do so. By staying above giving an opinion, you are sustaining a "mystique," and you make the interviewer keep trying to determine who you are. If the mystery of who you are is gone, the interviewer may go through the motions, but she has heard enough and has already formed an opinion. If you make the interviewer work to get insight into who you are, you sustain her interest and grow positively in her opinion because she is required to make judgments regarding who you are. The more the interviewer has to work to make those determinations, the more she develops a positive impression.

Be cognizant of industry positions on various issues, including support of government programs and pending legislation. If you are interviewing at a cosmetics firm that is strongly against animal testing, for example, you might think twice about wearing your fur-trimmed coat. This is all part of the organization profile that you should discover when researching recent news articles prior to your interview.

4.12   Would you like something to drink? A cigarette?

Some cultures use an offer of a drink as an opportunity to demonstrate hospitality. Others use it to determine the candidate's astuteness (the offer of a drink may be a test to determine the applicant's professional sophistication, because in some cultures a drink is accepted only after a relationship is established). Even if you want a cup of coffee (in fact, you are dying for one), pass on it politely. This is not a social call, and it might be just one more item to deflect your attention.

Some applicants, however, use the offer as one more indicator and opportunity to evaluate the organization. Whether it uses porcelain cups or Styrofoam, real milk or a chemical substitute, remember that you are there not to evaluate the quality of the beverage, but to get a job.

The issue of smoking in the office may be decided ahead of time by local statues and clean air laws. If you are traveling to another geographical area and are unaware of local statutes, observe the presence or lack of ashtrays and signage. One tobacco manufacturer has a "Thank You for Smoking" sign in the lobby! If you are a nonsmoker and the air is blue with smoke, you may have gotten your first indication of whether you wish to work in that environment. If you are a smoker, avoid partaking before the interview; the scent may proclaim your habit and could give the interviewer another issue to judge you on.

The same goes for other inquiries, such as, *"Where did you get that suit?" "Wow—what a great tan. Where did you go?" "I am so backed up [looking at a desk full of reports]—don't you just hate copiers?"*

Small talk can be a great assist in your job search and can be helpful regardless of the setting. Whether you are at the beginning of an interview or en route to an appointment, you never know when an opportunity may arise to uncover a job prospect through a casual conversation started with a person who just happens to be standing next to you. One comment may lead to another, and before you realize it (sly fox that you are), you have disclosed that you are looking for a job. The stranger, with whom you have just started the most casual of conversations, is aware of an open position. Not only might you pursue it, but you could ask to use his name (some organizations have formal employee referral programs).

BIG POINTS ABOUT SMALL TALK

❏ Small talk allows the interjection of the **human element** into what at times can be little more than a cattle call for applicants.

❏ The willingness of the interviewer to engage in any chitchat before the line of direct questions opens can be a strong indication of the **concern placed on the firm's employees**.

❏ If you are the slightest bit ill at ease with talking about "nothing," **practice**. Start light conversations on bank lines, at luncheons, while shopping, and in waiting rooms. You never know when you might uncover a terrific lead to a job opening.

❏ **Steer clear of controversial topics**, regardless of how the topic is introduced.

❏ **Stay focused on the purpose** of the interview while engaging in small talk, since you are there to discuss the job with you as the successful hire.

5

WHO ARE YOU?

For a long while, conventional thinking held that interviewers were supposed to stick to the straight and narrow when it came to what questions to ask a prospective candidate. (Civil rights legislation continues to be an ever-present reminder that employers can get into trouble when they stray from interview questions that are specifically and closely related to work.) Now, however, interviewers are interested in learning all that they can about every person they interview, not only as part of a due diligence process, but also to determine whether the candidate has the can do/will do/fit factors to do the job (while at the same time keeping the guidelines of employment laws in mind). Just as there are guides to preparing for interview questions, there is an ever-growing list of tactics, approaches, and questions that interviewers "should" ask in order to identify the "right" hire.

Interviewers have a responsibility to their employers to obtain as much information about you as you are willing to provide. By seeing your likes and dislikes and by finding out about other non-business-related issues, they have a better understanding of what you are about—both on and off the job. To clear the air, off-the-job issues should be restricted to those matters that are relevant to work. For example, a mother who is returning to work may make a convincing case that while she was away from her career, she was involved in major projects, as a volunteer for a not-for-profit, that enhanced her expertise in projects related to the job she is applying for. A career changer who has obsolete technical skills related to the manufacturing job that he just held needs to share his construction and automotive repair skills when considering new career opportunities.

Personal questions are intended to allow the interviewer to get to understand another dimension of your makeup.

What has brought you into this particular interviewer's office?

How has your job search been going?

How had your career progressed up until this point?

What are your feelings about this organization and this position?

Measuring Your EQ

An important ingredient for life success, first highlighted in 1995 and followed up with a stream of books by Daniel Goleman and other authors, is emotional intelligence (EQ) [Daniel Goleman, *Emotional Intelligence* (Bantam)]. *Interpersonal skills are needed* to know and understand what you and others around you are feeling and to know how to handle those feelings skillfully; when you are thinking in terms of street smarts and book smarts, add in "work smarts."

> *How do you motivate others? Can you empathize with customers, clients, supervisors, and fellow workers? Can you see another's point of view? When things get tough, boring, hectic, or chaotic at work, how do you react, and how do you help others to manage their feelings? Can you defuse emotionally charged situations? Do you know what makes you happy? Do you know what makes others feel satisfied or challenged?*

Even before the term *emotional intelligence* was coined, employers knew that merely having the intellectual intelligence or the skill to perform a job was not sufficient. Some experts even go so far as to attach negative emotional attributes, such as "cold," "calculating," "condescending," "inhibited," or "fastidious," to individuals with high IQs. On the other hand, individuals with high emotional abilities are seen as being "cheerful," "sympathetic," "responsible," "ethical," or "committed" because they appear to be happy with themselves and the people they associate with. One need only watch *The Office* or *The Big Bang Theory* on TV to see a variety of EQs (and total lack of same) in office environments!

This emotional intelligence translates into better communication skills on the job. Others want to work with and for people who understand them and who are able to support them. If a worker with a high EQ has a problem, she is more likely to attract others to help solve the problem than someone with a low EQ. *One thing that you are selling is your ability to solve problems,* not just physical problems (coming up with a better mousetrap), but interpersonal problems as well (assembling a team that develops a better mousetrap is likely to solve future problems as well).

Even if interviewers are not on the cutting edge of this philosophical theory, they know that the organization needs individuals who work well together. The employment puzzle needs a good fit, and personal questions are needed to find out what type of fit you would make.

To relate your EQ to the position and organization that you are interviewing for, refer to the "Personal Worksheet" (see pages 44–46) that you completed earlier. Looking at the first section ("What I Am Like"), list on the "On-the-Job EQ Worksheet" (see below) the specific attributes that you feel the organization associates with the position. For example, a supervisor of programmers might need to be "objective," "adaptable," "efficient," and "hardworking" for a position at a software developer whose business is just taking off (a baby Microsoft, perhaps). A possible question could be: "Give a specific example from your experience when you needed to be objective."

When one of the designs I was working on was having problems, I had to refer it to another department to review the specs. The problem turned out to be not in the design, but in a faulty component. Had I not referred it out but kept tinkering to fix it myself, it would have taken longer to resolve the problem.

ON-THE-JOB EQ WORKSHEET

Organization: _____

Position: _____

Personal Attributes Needed for This Position	Specific Example of When/Where You Exhibited This Attribute

*5.1 Tell me about yourself.

Whenever it is asked during an interview, this is a terrible "question" because it can trip up the unprepared. If it is going to be used at all, it is usually asked at the beginning of the formal part of the interview (and after the small-talk/introductory phase). In some circumstances other than a job interview, it is a great opener (e.g., for counseling interviews in a highly nondirected setting), but this interviewing approach requires highly trained and seasoned interviewers to be utilized most effectively. It is very likely that interviewers who use this approach:

- Are behind in the work that they had hoped to complete this day and have just remembered a commitment to conduct this interview and/or have forgotten what they did with your résumé and other paperwork.
- Have read somewhere in a magazine a superficial article that this is a great way to start an interview and have decided to try the question.
- Consider an interview to be a "test" of mettle and want to put applicants in the "hot seat" with a stress question up front.

Job seekers tell us that they sometimes experience a variation of this technique, especially when they are interviewing for a job that starts with a training program. "Tell me, starting with school, and progressing through the jobs that you have held, what you have been doing. Include any accomplishments, and bring me up to the present." Or, "What can you tell me about yourself that is *not* on your résumé?" Even if this approach is used and the person you are facing seems experienced, don't be lulled into thinking that he is any more prepared to turn your data into useful information than in the above other scenarios.

Knowing how to respond is important, and doing so in two minutes or less is essential. More than two minutes increases the possibility of your either boring the interviewer or losing her attention. In case this doesn't bother you, consider what you might have to do to awaken an interviewer who is fast asleep!

Take the time before the meeting to plan a script that you prepare precisely for such occasions. Here are some sample answers for different scenarios:

If you are reentering the job market after a time away:

I have experience in both the not-for-profit and the business sectors, primarily on a project basis. While I have been away from salaried positions the past few years to give attention to personal matters, I have frequently been involved in community-based projects that enhanced my business skills and will make me more effective as an employee on the business side once again. Let me give you one example that will demonstrate what I mean.

For a simple job change—no career change, no market reentry:

After starting a career with [name of organization] as a management trainee and rising up the career ladder there, I accepted an offer from ____ to work in its ___ division. I am now looking for a position with you because of the firm's decision to close that location.

For a career change:

After graduating from XYZ University with an engineering degree, I accepted a position with ABC Corporation to work for its ___ division. After five years of increased responsibility on a variety of projects, I was recruited by DEF, Inc., to be part of its new division specializing in ___. Now I am here because, as you may know, DEF has reconsidered its commitment to this area and has shut down that activity.

I have always been someone who enjoys meeting people and learning about their business; everyone likes to talk about their business. Sales is just another facet of those discussions—what do customers need, and how can I help them solve their problems? And I consider myself very fortunate to both like what I do and be rather good at it. Let me share some recent results.

Practice your response until you have an answer that you are comfortable with that takes about two minutes. After you give your answer, be quiet and wait for a response. There are also great opportunities to give similar brief presentations when you are introducing yourself at professional gatherings or other events where your profile and job search can be a subject of conversation. In these cases a shorter version—no longer than thirty seconds —is more effective.

*5.2 Why did you choose this time to leave your current/past position?

Be consistent in your answer. Consider any reasons that you may have included in your cover letter, in other conversations, on your application, and, if you were referred to the organization, in your conversation with the person who referred you. In addition, if you are still employed or are on speaking terms with your former employer, it is best to have that person give the same story for why you are no longer employed in case of reference checks. It is a small world, and it is not a difficult task to corroborate your account. (It is always helpful, if possible, to ask your former employer what potential employers will be told when they call. Try to get the statement in writing. If you already left, ask anyway. It is never too late to obtain a statement or written recommendation, and, in fact, time may have healed any wound that was felt on your departure.)

What matters almost as much as the specific answer that you give to this question is the tone and nonverbal gestures that you use while you are giving that answer. You need to be comfortable and confident with the answer that you give, regardless of what you say. If you have been fired for whatever reason, speak cautiously. *Never lie, but remember that you have control over what you say and how you say it.* Unless you have a real neophyte for an interviewer, he has probably heard all the stories already. You can certainly put a positive spin on any situation by describing how you learned from this development in your professional life.

If you are currently employed, the question might be phrased, "What is it about your current position that makes you feel that you would like to go elsewhere?" You can generate an answer with a positive spin by mentioning:

- *Industry-wide changes.* "New technology is making the organization's product obsolete." "It is no secret that the company will be phasing out production."
- *Organizational circumstances.* "The organization is restructuring/going out of business . . . has been acquired/merged/spun off." "New management is in the process of bringing in a new team from overseas."
- *Geographical relocation.* "The organization is leaving the area." "My spouse/significant other/partner requires a physical move and therefore I am looking for new employment."
- *Personal concerns.* "Organizationally I have gone as far as I could. The person above me is just two years older than I am, and there is nowhere else for her to go at this time." Do not take the *"I've learned all that I could"* approach. That contains a strong hint of *"I am concerned only about me, and you need to keep me in a learning mode."* If that is what interviewers hear (whether that is an accurate reading of your comments or not), they may take that to mean, *"If you hire me, you will have a problem because if you don't keep giving me learning opportunities, I will look elsewhere."*
- *Legal forms of harassment.* Mentioning forms of harassment other than sexual, while not illegal, serves to disclose to persons meeting with you that you have had problems with your previous employers and to risk spreading ill will. Will they think that hiring you is worth the risk? Harassment could include being threatened with termination for refusing to work overtime, bullying by a supervisor that seemed to be condoned by the organization, or using harsh tones, a boisterous voice, or vulgar language

as part of the ongoing terms and conditions of employment. Teasing or threats by supervisors or peers, for whatever reason, may be valid reasons for your leaving your last employer. *"Unprofessional behavior"* would be a good brief statement. Another might be, *"The atmosphere was just like high school again—something I thought I had left behind a while ago."*

5.3 Had you thought of leaving your current/past position before? If so, what held you there?

Good interviewers ask this question. They are attempting to learn your motivation and your ability to consider a course of action and then take it. There is a theory in the recruiting industry that is accepted as fact (and the few studies that have been conducted to determine its accuracy tend to corroborate it): that anyone who considers and accepts an offer and then takes a counteroffer from his current organization will be out of his current organization within 18 months.

There had been phenomenal growth in the industry, and _____ Company rode the crest of the wave. I was proud to be part of the product development team, but recent market adjustments have not resulted in any changes. I have so many ideas and am anxious to make contributions to a growing company such as yours; I have been excited by the new products you have recently introduced.

5.4 Are you looking for a permanent or a temporary job?

This is a "gotcha" question. If you say the wrong thing, the interviewer knocks you out of the box. In the not too distant past, it used to be simple. There were those who were looking for permanent jobs, and then there was a very small group who really preferred a "temp" job because of their unique personal or professional needs. Actors wanted temporary work so that they would be able to audition for parts whenever they were called upon to do so. Others who might have sought "temp" jobs included those between circumstances: someone who was waiting for a spouse to be settled in a new location, a student who was waiting to return to school, and professional jockeys were some examples.

All that has changed. More people are now seeking temporary employment in order to allow them to pursue other interests, which may be income-producing or not. Another group of people are working temporary jobs involuntarily—that is, because they are unable to secure regular full-time employment, at time cobbling together several jobs or assignments to make up one full-time paycheck.

Notice too that the term *regular* was just used. More often than not, employers are avoiding the word *permanent* as a description for a type of job. They usually do this on the advice of counsel, who feels that by having a category of employee known as *permanent*, the employer may be inadvertently establishing a contractual obligation.

If you are interested only in temporary work and you say so, interviewers may dismiss your application because they need employees who are willing to stay. On the other hand, if the interviewer wants to hire employees on a contingency basis, and you say that you want a permanent job, then the interviewer may lose interest in you.

If a permanent job is what you truly want, you do not lose by stating your preference directly. You can also show your astuteness by adding, *"Although I ideally would like a regular full-time job, I would be willing to be considered for a temporary position if that is all that is available because I would really like to work for this organization."* The tag-on at the end of your statement should grab the attention of the interviewer because you seem flexible and are interested in the organization. Consider your answer carefully beforehand because it gives your potential employer the opportunity to delay an offer of a "regular job," since you are already agreeing to a "look and see" approach. In the current job environment, part-time and temporary jobs frequently become regular and full-time when economic circumstances improve.

5.5　How do you feel about looking for another job?
Pragmatic, positive, and proactive is the way to go.

> *I have to be honest and say that I would have been more than happy to remain with _____ for a few more years, as there were goals that I still sought to reach, but once the firm was acquired, a new team of managers was brought in. So, even though it was not my idea to leave, now that I am out here looking, I am excited. This opportunity to work here at _____ would not have arisen otherwise.*

Take a positive, upbeat approach. *"Looking for another job is an opportunity."* Or, *"I don't have to look for another job. I do it so that I can continue to grow professionally."* What the interviewer hopes to hear is that you are taking charge of your own destiny. You are not looking at her firm because you have little or no choice. You need to demonstrate that you are in control and a go-getter, and that even when circumstances deal you a harsh hand, you look for the upside.

5.6　I see that you worked for _____ for _____ years; how does it feel to be back in the job market? How did you prepare yourself for this job search?
Again, stress the positives and move on to the next subject.

It feels a little like leaving home for the first time—but in a good way. Staying there for ___ years was great, but once I had made the decision to leave, the energy just came to me to embrace this as a great move. Checking out industry leaders, I rediscovered your company and was excited to see this job opening.

*5.7 What has been the extent of your job search so far? How long have you been looking?

The longer you have been looking for a job, the weaker you will appear to interviewers because they will wonder why it is taking you so long. What is worse is the perception that if no one is interested in hiring you, what are they doing spending time with you?

If you have been looking for a while and you want to admit it, or if you have to confirm it because of the dates on your résumé, then give it a positive spin. You have been looking for so long because you want to be careful about your next career move. You have had offers, but nothing "rang the bell." If you take this route, be really ready to discuss the offers that you have rejected, because it is such an obvious opener that it begs for the "next" question. You may even anticipate an additional question regarding how you were spending your time when you were unemployed by offering that you wanted to brush up on your skills, so you took the initiative to invest in classes or workshops.

5.8 What career options do you feel that you have at this moment? What have you done to explore them?

To mention one or more alternatives here (in addition to the one that you are discussing with the interviewer) is to risk the interviewer's perception either that you are not that interested in the position being discussed or that you are unfocused. There is an exception: suppose you are beginning your career and are meeting with a human resources recruiter from an organization that offers several career options for entry-level college and graduate-level employees on a management track. In such a case, you can mention more than one option. For example, someone with a degree in finance and global management might be considering either a domestic investment banking position or one in the international division. If you share that information with anyone in the organization, remember to stay consistent throughout the interview process in the organization. With luck, both groups may fight for you, and the offer that you take should not limit your going forward. Consider the recruitment meetings as networking opportunities, and try to maintain those contacts as you move through the organization in your chosen career track.

When possible, open up the idea that you have many different facets.

In my career in finance, I have worked in both budgeting and cash flow management. Although I am coming from a management position in a budget department, I feel that managing your cash flow would play to my strengths and would be a job in which I could really add value to the organization.

5.9 What are you looking for in a job? What would be your ideal job? Your ideal employer? Your ideal career?

Briefly put, describe a situation that shows you and the organization as linked. Consider what this organization is and "paint" yourself into the picture. For example, *"I am looking for a position where I can make a meaningful contribution continuously and grow professionally." "I have always hoped to have a positive impact on the environment; I know you are a 'green' company, and I admire your position on _____ and already am excited over the opportunity to support these operations."* You may also consider the best job you ever had to confirm your thoughts on this question before the meeting. Of course, having a positive correlation between this response and the job that the organization has open is a necessity.

5.10 Describe a major goal that you have recently set for yourself. What are you doing to attain it?

Select a meaningful project that is either personal or professional in nature. "Complete my education" is one. "Find the right job" is another. The second is preferable because it brings the discussion back to the topic you are there to discuss—a job for you in this specific organization. To portray this as a major goal once again leaves no doubt about the fact that you are very serious about a career and a job with the organization. This is a statement that does not hurt, no matter how often you make it.

Other than the obvious "Find the right position," I have also taken steps to complete a master's program. It may take some time, but I feel that being a lifelong learner can only benefit both me and my employer.

5.11 Describe the best boss/supervisor that you ever had. Describe the worst. What was the best job that you ever had? The worst?

When you are preparing yourself for this meeting and the job search, consider whom you most enjoyed working for as a boss. On a sheet of paper, describe the qualities that that person possessed that affected his ability to be effective with you and the other members of the team. While you are at it, describe the qualities of the worst person you ever worked for. Compare your two lists of qualities and see what separates them. It is likely that your best boss's ability to deal with people was linked with her ability to get the job done—namely, to be sensitive to the needs and personalities of people.

When you are asked this question at your meeting, you are then ready to briefly describe the situation and speak genuinely about the boss. If you have not thought about it before the meeting, you will have to pause while you reflect on who your best boss was and then consider what to say before saying it. This is a tough task, given the circumstances and pressures of a job interview. Again, if the qualities and type of management style mirror those that you feel the organization aspires to attract, you have scored major points.

> *It is odd, but my worst job and my best boss were at the same place. One summer I worked doing litter collection along a major public beach; my boss had worked there for decades and was a walking history of the area. I learned so much about local history and geology that whenever I take my family to the beach now, I share these stories and my love of the area with them.*

*5.12 How do you feel about your career progress to date? If your prior employer had not had to do massive layoffs, what do you think your career progress there would have been?

When you are defining your career objectives and evaluating your progress to date in the confines of an interview, you should deal frankly with this question. Regardless of the answer that you share and the answer that perhaps you keep to yourself at this interviewing session, demonstrate satisfaction up to a point, and that point is your reason for deciding to move on in this direction now.

> *At _____, there was an overseas rotation for middle managers who were being considered for senior positions. I was slotted for the next round of rotation and was looking forward to being promoted to head my department.*

5.13 How do you define success? Has your definition changed as a result of recent economic events?

This is another personal query that you should consider your answer to before the meeting, not so much for the interviewer's sake as for your own. In the meeting, however, you need to realize that the person who is asking the question is asking it in an organizational—not a career counseling—context. You may consider linking *recognition* to *meaningful contribution* as an answer: *"I define success as being able to provide for my family financially while performing work that is tied to the success of the organization that employs me."*

Success is the ability to meet your goals . . . and knowing how to set the "right" goals and establish a plan for achieving them.

5.14 Which of your personal characteristics do you think will be needed to be a success in this position?

As a librarian, a good memory, a sense of curiosity, and a genuine interest in people are three traits that have supported my career to date. A willingness to learn and to adapt to new technology and methods is essential also.

As with many of the other answers of this type, you need to show that you understand both what the position requires AND what are your prime personal selling points that uniquely qualify you for the position. Your earlier research and self-analysis again proves valuable.

5.15 What would you hope to accomplish in your first six months if we were to hire you?

When the question is phrased this way, you need to answer in terms of results. From the work you have already completed in filling out your "Personal Worksheet," (see pages 44–46) and your "On-the-Job EQ Worksheet" (see page 66), this should not be a difficult question for you to address at the interview. Review your list of attributes thoroughly before the meeting because you want to be sure that you do not take this topic for granted. Persistence, loyalty, a strong work ethic, strong communication skills, results orientation, team player, and insatiable curiosity are among the characteristics that may be included; they are accepted in any work environment and certainly could be used for starters. Be ready to provide instances where you put to use any of these characteristics mentioned for the possibility of follow-up questions.

Watch out for "multitasking." There is some backlash that moves the emphasis to "one thing at a time is best."

Much of the interview process can be boiled down to "You need _____, and I can provide _____."

From your description of the position, I feel that the most essential characteristics are flexibility and persistence—if staying extra hours is needed, I can certainly do that—and as for being creative, looking for ways to assist the customers, and not giving up, well, that is something that I am very familiar with.

5.16   If you could, what would you change about this position?

Consider the source of the question. If it comes from someone in human resources or recruiting, it may be "filler"—a question that the interviewer may have heard about, even though she has no actual insider knowledge of the position. If it comes from a line manager or your would-be supervisor, he is tapping your brain to get some free consulting or wants to see if you are already planning to change things before you are even offered the job. Don't be tempted. Unless something is truly glaring, you would be best advised to say, *"Until I am actually in the position and see what works and what doesn't, I would be hard pressed to make any recommendations."*

*5.17 What do you like the most about this position? What do you like the least about this position?

This question usually has two parts, which come one at a time. The setup comes with first asking you what you like best because it is the easier of the two questions. (If you cannot think of any positives, why are you there?) To answer what you like the most, identify two or three major job elements or characteristics that really are the essence of the job:

> *"I like the amount of time that will be devoted to outside clients."*
>
> *"I particularly like the problem-solving elements of the position."*
>
> *"The team that I would be working with looks terrific."*

When you are asked to identify the least attractive aspects of the position, try to avoid the question by saying, *"I can't think of anything that I dislike about the position,"* or, *"It sounds just like what I had hoped it would be."* Appear confident and knowledgeable about the position. Then try to share something that the interviewer has already mentioned about it so that you are seen as an empathizing, perceptive, and good listener. Or come up with an obvious, minor drawback:

The only thing that might make the position a difficult one is the two-block distance between the department's location and the group it is expected to serve. How does the current staff deal with it?

5.18   Do you prefer delegation or hands-on control? What is your management style?

The interviewer is trying to determine the fit between your approach to the organization's environment. If you prefer delegation, you need to build a mutual feeling of trust in your subordinates. Hands-on control demands a different approach by you and by each subordinate. If you have any insight into the organization's managerial style, you can structure your response. You should answer this question directly and openly, because, if the situation requires a real delegating manager and you happen to be real hands-on, the fit is not a good one unless you are really flexible. Even then, the chances are that, if you are hired, you will revert to your old management style when the pressure mounts, and that could spell disaster.

I have had diverse groups to manage, and I have found that some respond to a "show and tell" style, while others appreciate having more responsibility parceled out. My innate style is delegation, but I have been flexible as needs have presented themselves.

5.19   What kind of people do you like to work with? What do you feel is the easiest type of person to deal with? The most difficult?

These three relationship questions seek to determine what makes for an easy personal interaction for you. Do you prefer the direct, hands-on approach, or do you look instead for the person who just gives you an enormous amount of autonomy? To be prepared for any of these questions, determine whom

- You are best able to deal with.
- You have had to deal with organizationally, and have found best to work for and with.
- You have had the greatest difficulty working with.

To take a comprehensive approach and to be sure that you are identifying every possible type of person you have had to interact with at work, think up, down, and at the same level. If you are hit with any of these questions, be prepared to answer all three of them.

"What is the most difficult type of person to work with?" is not as easy to deal with as the other two questions. But do not become worried or defensive, because this is really a gift question. Try to identify annoying characteristics that are typically abhorred:

>*"The person who refuses to stay when asked to help solve a problem."*
>
>*"Fellow workers who consistently work at a pace that just barely keeps them employed."*
>
>*"Someone who tries to avoid responsibility for deadlines."*
>
>*"People who have no passion for their work."*

If you agree that one or more of these types are the worst, then you have your answer.

5.20   What is your prime short-term personal goal?

A chance to show that you are not a one-dimensional candidate! Have you thought about learning a foreign language or running a 10K race? Or doing some volunteer work with children in your area? The key is to pick something that is not so totally absorbing that the interviewer will question whether you will have time to work, but to show that you can think outside of the 9 to 5 environment and are willing to invest in yourself. Honesty is appreciated here—if you are hired, you may be asked at a later date, "How is the running coming along?"

*5.21 What are your strong points? What are your weak points?

Take this opportunity to share your strong points with the interviewer, stressing qualities that are relevant for the position at hand and also important to you. Loyalty, a strong work ethic, good interpersonal and communications skills, and a project and results orientation are all characteristics that interviewers love to hear. Be prepared to give examples that illustrate one or more of your personal characteristics; there very well might be a follow-up question that asks for an example.

These questions often travel on the heels of each other. Do not be as open about your weaknesses as you are about your strong points. Try to identify qualities (or their lack) that are not so relevant to the position being discussed. The interviewer is interested in your ability to self-critique as well as in what actions you do take to improve.

>*"I must admit that I am a workaholic."*
>
>*"I am impatient with others who display no sense of urgency."* (If you use something like this, you may be asked how you deal with people like this, or how you improve their performance.)

Or damn yourself with faint praise:

"I always try to come in ahead of deadlines."
A better tack might be to name something that you are working on:

I have always been reticent about speaking in public, so a few months ago I registered for a public speaking class. I already feel that I am more comfortable in front of the class. I am the first to admit that I am not yet a top-notch speaker, but my confidence is definitely growing, and I no longer dread the opportunity to present.

5.22 What is your greatest accomplishment? List your five most significant accomplishments.

If possible, keep your answer focused on work. *"Convincing management to proceed with this multimillion dollar project—and making it work"* is a grand answer if you have such a situation to draw upon. Most of us, though, do not have that luxury and must select more mundane and perhaps boring subjects instead. A careful review of your past experiences should provide the preparation necessary to field this question in the most effective manner.

If you cannot find a work-related situation, identify a situation that is comparable to one that might occur at work. Practice being a good storyteller. People love brief, interesting stories. The restoration of a house, completing college, or raising a family would certainly qualify. The more you are able to confine the discussion to work-related issues, however, the more interviewers will see information that they consider strong evidence that you are a person who gets things done. To the extent that you can quantify your answer with facts (increased sales X percent, raised X dollars in donations, worked on a project that took X months), tell what your role was (leader, team member), and explain why this was an important accomplishment (what the end result was for the organization), you will have shown great acumen in your response.

Even though I was only a junior account officer, one of my accounts was awarded a huge contract that required installment financing and working with a team of lenders. I jumped in, worked weekends, and put together a package that enabled us to be the lead bank. In the end, the customer paid the loan in full, all according to terms.

5.23 If we spoke to your current/former boss, what would he or she say are your greatest strengths/your greatest weaknesses?

These questions may be a sign of an inexperienced interviewer or of an ineffective or poor listener who is asking formula questions and not paying attention to the answers. Go back to your earlier answers on personal strengths and highlight a few that were associated with your most recent position. As to weaknesses, you must not say, *"My boss would say that she has a difficult time identifying any weaknesses in my current position."* If you do, you have avoided the question successfully, but that "victory" also means that interviewers are repulsed or frustrated in their attempt to get a discussion going. This is not a move without consequences. Your interviewer may ponder whether your evasiveness is a pattern (and determine that you are not someone whom the organization should pursue further). You could point out something that you learned or overcame that used to be a weakness.

I used to be a worker who always wanted to complete every project perfectly. I have learned to determine appropriate quality standards and be realistic about each project's importance in the context of the variety of tasks and projects that I am responsible for.

5.24 What features did you like the least/the most about your current/last position?

This is a great question for both you and the interviewer. For you, it is great (provided you are prepared) because it gives you the opportunity to demonstrate how you perceive work. Just be careful to stay focused and brief. Go back to the "Job History Worksheet" in Chapter 3 (see page 41) and see what items you can highlight. *Obviously, the aspects that you like least are what have brought you to this interview, and the features that you like best are those that have kept you at that job up to now and are similar to those that you might find here.* Select features on your least-liked lists that probably do not exist at the new organization (or ones that it would not espouse), and select as the ones that you liked those that coincidentally are also part of the new position! For example, do not extol the foreign travel opportunities at your prior employer when you are interviewing at a solely domestic firm. And, if you praise the "old" job too much, you may beg the question: if it was/is so great, why did you leave?

5.25 What will you do if this position is not offered to you?

This is a silly question, but treat it seriously if it is asked. Act disappointed but professional.

Since this interview seems to be going smoothly and my qualifications appear to satisfy the job requirements, I would be curious as to what area of inquiry was not satisfactory. Since I am very impressed with this organization, I would ask for some feedback and whether I could be considered for other similar positions in the future.

5.26 Where do you hope to be professionally in five years?

This is one of those standard questions that someone thought up years ago and that for some reason has continued to grow in popularity. It is not a bad question because it is open-ended with a timeline. The applicant is expected to provide a realistic answer that portrays neither a lust for power *("I want to be your boss")* nor a lack of focus and ambition *("I want to be right where I am, or win the lottery and spend the rest of my life watching TV")*. Instead, the candidate is expected to show bridled ambition (except in a few organizations that might seek to see a "killer" attitude):

I hope to continue to be with this organization in a position of increased responsibility where I will be able to continue my professional growth while making an ongoing corporate contribution to the organization's continued success.

5.27 Would you consider volunteering or interning at our organization?

Be wary. First of all, only not-for-profits are legally allowed to take volunteers. There is the minimum wage law to consider. I mention this not to cause a conflict with the organization that is raising the question, but to make sure that you consider the offer in light of your own interest. These days, some employers in several industries in the private sector accept "interns" for unpaid positions, and there are takers at that price. Consider whether accepting a nonpaying job in the hope of getting a paying one later enhances your value to a potential employer. Be careful, because frequently a perception goes with your salary level, bluntly stated as, *"You get what you pay for."*

Keep in mind also that the time that you spend as a volunteer is time that you are not spending looking for a job. There is a trade-off between your time and attendant costs in working for "free" and the ability to get your foot in the door and receive on-the-job training. This tactic might be more valuable when you are considering a career change or an entry-level position. To show interest in the organization but discourage your being thought of as free labor, try saying

I would jump at the chance to be part of your organization, but unfortunately my financial situation precludes my forgoing a salary at this point.

5.28 Do you think you are creative? Do others think you are creative?

Different jobs demand different amounts of creativity. If you are a copywriter in an ad agency, you are required to take blank pieces of paper and type out thoughts that not only are creative but also reflect the product or service that you are being paid to advertise. If you are a supervisor in a bookkeeping department, creativity is not highly valued. A creative person may not be a valid match for a position dealing with debits and credits and journal entries. *Determine the kinds and level of creativity that are inherent in the open position, and offer examples from your experience that complement them.*

*5.29 How would you describe your own personality?

Review the first section of the "Personal Worksheet" (see pages 44–46) that you completed earlier to choose the adjectives that are "you." Do not be afraid to use a dictionary or thesaurus to be absolutely certain about various shades of meaning.

There is no reason for you to do this alone. Ask friends, family members, and business associates what words could be used to describe you. In many cases, friends are delighted to help with your job search in any capacity. *Ask yourself what kind of personality is needed to fill the position, and cite your characteristics that support your candidacy.*

*5.30 May I have your business card?

If you have portrayed yourself as a consultant, this could be a pop quiz. Your business card is an essential tool, and the quality of the card (texture, logo, and print) is part of the statement that you are making. Even if you are not consulting, it is a good idea to have a card and offer it, whether or not the question is asked. It is perfectly polite and correct to ask for a card at the end of the meeting if one has yet to be offered. When you offer one of yours in exchange for the interviewer's, you are reciprocating—a warm, friendly, and totally professional gesture. However, don't do as one job applicant did and give the interviewer a business card identifying yourself as a member of an occult group specializing in witchcraft or one with a strange e-mail address such as hotchick76@aol.com.

WHEN THE SPOTLIGHT IS ON YOU

❑ **Do not contradict yourself.** Let your nonverbal message match your sales pitch; act confident, and highlight your past successes and current skills. If you are selling yourself as traditional and conservative because that is appropriate for the industry or organization that you are seeking to work in, make sure that both the appearance of your résumé and your personal presentation echo this. "You on paper" should be the same person as "you at the interview."

❑ **Do not let your guard down** when you are faced with questions that you may think are "soft." Be prepared with crisp, focused responses.

❑ **Sell your interpersonal skills.** Show how easy and great you would be to work with or for.

❑ **Enlist the help of family members, friends, and peers** with your self-analysis; identify your "best" and "worst" points.

❑ **Continue to grow personally and professionally.** Read, take classes, meet with fellow professionals, network, or attend seminars. Keep yourself sharp and current.

❑ **Form a "success team"** of several trusted friends (not coworkers) to meet periodically to discuss career strategies.

6

WORK SMARTS

A recent magazine article stated that *the single most important career fact to remember is that you need to constantly reinvent yourself and your career.* In this competitive market, it is not the "know it all" who attracts the best offers, but the individual who is constantly learning. Learning in classrooms, learning on the job, and life experience all point favorably toward job applicants who can grow with the organization and be dynamic in their positions.

Interviewers are interested in your professional education: what do you know about the industry, their organization, the position, and your relationship to the future of their organization, and how did you discover all this information? They are seeking to determine how professionally skilled and developed you are. How do you learn—what kind of learning curve can they expect if they hire you? When might you start making a contribution? Where are you intellectually? How much research into their business have you done? Have you been learning and growing over the past 10 years, or have you been doing the same things in the same way during that time period? It is surprising how many candidates show up for interviews not knowing very much about the company—its products, history, competition, and industry. With free access to information online or at libraries, there really is little excuse for not doing some basic research.

While we are on the topic, your research should not just be for the benefit of wowing the interviewer. Hopefully, you, our reader, also realize the value of research to you, which is even more important in this process. It is exciting to watch consumers use the Internet to obtain all the information they feel they need before they make an important purchase—and then spend more time searching for the Web site that offers the best price. How much more important is it for you to find out all you can about the next job you are trying to land to make sure that you know exactly (or at least as much as possible) what you are getting?

If you go into an interview thinking that the questions that may be asked will be concentrated solely on subject matter that is directly related to the jobs that you have had and the schools that you have attended, you will be unprepared for the questions in this chapter, which may very well be included during the course of your meeting.

The "Knowledge Worker" and the Postindustrial Era

The "knowledge worker" as a concept is becoming ever more widely accepted by organizations as an accurate portrayal of what the postindustrial-era corporation requires. In fact, the preference for the knowledge worker is becoming so widely and frequently accepted that it is often even applied to the assembly-line worker in manufacturing. With that growing acceptance of the concept, the worker with "knowledge skills" is becoming increasingly in demand in the workplace.

BECOME A LIFELONG LEARNER BECAUSE

❏ **Change** is more and more a factor in any profession.

❏ **Continuing education is perceived to be more effective** than the more traditional "get a degree and be done with it" approach.

❏ **Careers are constantly in flux.** Some careers become obsolete seemingly overnight, and their industry along with them.

❏ **The expectation of one "career for life" is unreasonable,** and employers realize that shifting markets make the smart candidate one who can "reinvent" herself as needed.

One more comment: remember Webinars and online education. It is easier than ever to economically learn new skills or enhance those that you have already acquired—regardless of where you live and work. Many Webinars or podcasts are free, and although online universities charge tuition, there is financial aid available, and you never have to worry about getting to class! Since the classes are virtual, you are in control of when you "go to class" by turning on your computer and checking into the Web site. Additionally, engaging in any of the online alternatives that we suggest here demonstrates not only that you are a lifelong learner, but also that you are an e-learner—involved in state-of-the-art learning opportunities. The Internet allows you to obtain the highest-quality education available anywhere. MIT, for instance, offers free online courses for any takers. The only catch is that you can't take the courses for credit—a small price to pay!

To review everything that you do "know" and your educational history, complete the "Education Worksheet" (see below). Do not neglect to list any on-the-job training, seminars or workshops that you may have attended, or classes that you may be currently taking or enrolled in. Which of these you disclose as

EDUCATION WORKSHEET

Provide details for each school or academic experience listed on your résumé, starting with the current or most recent. *Note:* Your college details are less crucial the longer you have been working since graduation. The more recent your graduation, the more likely it is that you will be asked about your educational experience.

Name of school: _____

Address: _____

Telephone number: _____

URL: _____

Date started: _____

Major courses of study: _____

Degree received (or anticipated): _____

Date graduated (or expected): _____

Academic honors/awards: _____

Courses that relate to your job search: _____

Names of contacts who might still be there and may remember you:

_____

Why did you choose this school? _____

_____

Why did you choose this course of study? _____

_____

If you are a recent graduate, name, e-mail address, and telephone number of academic reference: _____

_____

Graduate school? Thesis/dissertation topic: _____

Future academic plans: _____

Seminars/workshops (dates, location/sponsor, and subject):

_____

_____

_____

being relevant to the job opening is certainly under your control. Do not neglect any classes or seminars that you may have taught.

Knowledge, of course, is not limited to instructional situations; review the third section ("What I Know") of the "Personal Worksheet" (see pages 44–46) to remind yourself of hidden skills. Again, if you are applying for a job as an administrative assistant, you may not wish to disclose your secretarial skills. Consider what skills or types of knowledge are necessary for this position (and for future advancement), and list these on the "On-the-Job IQ" form (see below). To be certain that you have these skills in your repertoire, write next to each skill or type of knowledge how you came by it or where you acquired it, including the date. For example, you may have knowledge of Quicken accounting software because you use it for your personal financial records, or you may be able to speak and

On the Job IQ

Organization: _____

Position: _____

Rate your level of proficiency:

1 = beginner   2 = experienced   3 = expert/able to teach others

Skills/Knowledge Needed for This Position	Specific Example of When and Where You Acquired This Skill/Type of Knowledge	Level

write Spanish as a result of a stint in the military. If either of these falls into the "that was a long time ago" category, determine what it will take to get you up to speed. Then use that determination in your decision as to whether you disclose that skill or not. If you decide to upgrade your knowledge/skill level, choosing to disclose that could be an important sign that you are a proactive lifelong learner. Of particular importance is your honesty in rating the level of proficiency you can offer the organization. Be up to date with your terminology; do not refer to the World Wide Web, Xeroxing copies, the girls, or mobile telephones.

6.1 If you could start your career over again, what would you do differently?

Knowing what happened to the company or industry that you started in, would you still have chosen to work for your first employer? This "road not taken" question may be a natural one if you were employed by a company that was in the news for failing or an industry that has had economic problems. It may be idle curiosity ("Gee, what was it like knowing that the company was going down the tubes?" or "Guess you never thought there would have been all these other media choices.") It could be an effort to determine your resilience in the face of uncontrollable issues. You must be careful not to sound wistful. Remember that you are dealing with a job interviewer, not a therapist. If you cannot think of anything, say, *"I am satisfied with my career and the direction it has taken"* or *"Even though the end result was traumatic for all involved, I have a lot of respect for the admirable way it was handled, and I learned a lot about how to handle myself in the face of adversity. The company tried to provide outplacement for the employees whenever possible."* Then, if you do think of anything you might have done differently, try to consider something that would have made your arrival at your current point swifter: *"I only wish that I had applied to this organization when I was starting."*

For career changers, this question is a great opportunity for you to volunteer that this is actually the reason that you are seeking the job you are in the organization you are meeting with. When the interviewer asks this question, this could be the first opportunity for you to jump in before you are asked more directly the reason that you are seeking the job you are seeking, given the unrelated experience you have had to date. It is to your advantage to disclose the information when you are free and wish to do so.

*6.2 What do you know about the position for which you are applying?

This is a good opportunity to clear the air. If you have a lot of information about the position, speak confidently and briefly. If you have little or no information, say so. *Rule of thumb: a little information is a better response than none.*

The information in the job listing was enough to interest me and allow me to feel that I could fulfill the function. I did look for similar positions online to find additional information, but I would rather hear how _____ views the position.

If you have no information about the position, the burden is on you to have a reason for applying for a position about which you know nothing—not an impossible situation, but usually somewhat odd. This is a question that you should ask yourself regularly as you go through the selection process, and salient facts should be marked on your "Organization Fact Sheet" (see page 50).

Although I was not able to obtain specific information about this position, being associated with your organization was so enticing that I knew I had to follow up. The position of _____ sounds very similar to the one I held at _____. Can you give me some details?

Do not forget that the purpose of the interview is to share information; do not be afraid to get additional information about the position if you need to. In fact, the absence of specific information about the position itself would be cause for concern.

Be careful, too, if you do know a lot about the position. What you know may be inaccurate because of the source of your information, or it may simply be that the parameters have changed. Where better to get more accurate and up-to-date information than from the person who will be your supervisor/manager?

IS THE POSITION FOR YOU?

❑ Make sure it is a position that you really want to pursue: **"will do."**
❑ Do you feel that you have the **"can do"** skills?
❑ Can you see yourself working here effectively? Will you **"fit"**?
❑ Flesh out your information concerning the position and the company in the course of the interview.

*6.3   What do you know about our company?
What do you know about our competition? About our products? Do you use our products? What is your overall impression of this position or organization? Based on your professional knowledge and instincts, you should be prepared for this question—whether or not the question is actually asked during the interview—

because you should have asked it of yourself. If subtitles were provided for these questions, they would be, "Why do you want this job?" and "Why do you want to work here?" Provide the interviewer with an answer that is not as frank or lengthy as the answer you may have come up with in discussions with yourself. This is an opportunity to show the depth of your knowledge and the reach of your contacts by sharing briefly what you have learned about the organization from the interview process and from all the information you have gathered about the organization and the position.

When I learned that you had this job opening, I remembered the article in [magazine/newspaper/Web site] regarding your "green" approach to production. I was impressed with your commitment to the environment.

Your products have been a household mainstay for as long as I can remember, and I can certainly say that your reputation has preceded this interview.

Part of your preparation should include kicking the tires. If at all possible, try the product or service before you meet with anyone at the company. This includes looking for ads and trying customer service—a key question to ask yourself is, will you be proud to be associated with this organization and the products it produces? You need to have a very positive response before you seek out the organization as a potential employer. This is not to say, however, that you are ready to marry the organization before your first meeting. Your interest in the organization should grow the more you get to experience the organization firsthand through on-site visits and meeting with key players.

*6.4   What is the most recent skill that you learned? What was the newest thing that you learned how to do? Where and when did you learn it?
The answer to this question is the essence of this chapter: *portray yourself as an interested, active, lifelong learner.* Try to avoid putting a time frame on your answer (unless you took a workshop just the other day). This question is a prime example of why it is important for you to prepare and to complete the various worksheets highlighting your work and education history. And, there could be the obvious follow-up questions.

As a member of _____, I get its newsletter, and it often runs weekend workshops. Whenever there is a new offering, I check it out. I have attended three so far this year, covering marketing and package design.

6.5 Why did you choose to learn that? Why did you seek to acquire that skill?

Since I spend so much time working on one, I felt that it was essential that I understand all the workings of all kinds of computers, including notebooks and laptops. I thought a class in computer repair would provide insights. And it has been fascinating.

6.6 How do you learn? What is your learning style (hands-on, research, or by example)?

This question gives you the opportunity to talk about yourself without any really right or wrong implications. With this question, interviewers are not, as it might seem, making a notation so that, if you are offered the job, you will be given training that is tailored to your most effective learning style. The question is asked more to determine whether you are able to learn quickly and be ready to perform immediately after the training program, regardless of its brevity.

It is best to present an action-oriented format that underscores that the best way to learn involves getting to practice wherever possible and then perform on the job immediately after any training is completed. There may be no opportunity to practice during the learning session, but this answer will show that you are an astute learner, and if practice is included in the training program, so much the better. The last element to mention, but not demand, is feedback. You like occasional feedback to ensure that you are putting what you have been trained to do into action correctly. Don't emphasize constant or regular feedback, because then the interviewer will see that you require constant attention—a problem!

My experience is that some skills, such as accounting, are best learned from books or software programs, whereas others require hands-on training, such as learning to drive. I think being presented with the information, combined with an opportunity to perform under some guidance, and then direct application works great for most skills.

*6.7 How do you keep informed professionally?

This question *assumes that you do keep informed professionally* and that you consider yourself a professional. What do you *read* on a daily basis? Weekly? Biweekly? Monthly? Quarterly? Depending on your field, a variety of materials are published on all these schedules. The "quarterlies" usually contain lengthy articles that provide serious, in-depth treatment of a topic. Notice that the first activity mentioned in response to the question is "read." Given the proliferation of TV, smartphones, and the Internet into every area of our lives, these electronic media frequently replace print media in the development of our intellectual skills, both personally and professionally. The more you grow in your profession, the more you are expected to pursue multiple sources of information that provide increasingly sophisticated data to regularly give breadth and depth to your knowledge base.

6.8   What professional organizations do you belong to? [Or, if an organization was mentioned on your résumé: Are you very active with _____ (group)?]

Being involved with your local group of professionals, chamber of commerce, or alumni association shows that you both have an active interest in the business world and make the effort to keep up to date. Do not exaggerate your involvement, as you have no idea what role your interviewer plays in these areas.

> *That is odd. I have attended the last three meetings of _____, and am sure I would have met you because it is a small group.*

Ouch—busted!

> *I follow its activities online and read its newsletters; I really miss being able to be more active, but I can't because of the time involved in my job search.*

YOUR RESOURCES REVEAL A LOT ABOUT YOU

❑ **The local library.** In this multimedia world, the library continues to be the greatest source of a lot of information, and since public libraries have embraced the Internet, they are great sources for databases for a variety of publications. The best part, since the information is electronic, is that you may not have to physically go to the library. It may be available from your personal computer and therefore never closes. All you may need to do is get a library card and register for online access.

❑ **Local newspapers** and business publications such as the *New York Times* and the *Wall Street Journal* (either print or online editions).

❑ **Professional publications and newsletters.**

❑ **Cable and broadcast media.**

❑ **Electronic media** such as the Internet, RSS feeds, digital newsletters, and podcasts.

❑ **Professional associates:** unions, associations, conventions, conferences, seminars, workshops.

❑ **Corporate, industry, and government agency Web sites.**

*6.9   What have you learned from the jobs that you have held?

This is an opportunity for you to *summarize your experience from a learning perspective*. Complete and review your "Experience Worksheet" (see pages 101–102) to see what skills and accomplishments you have developed from job to job. Mention both the task aspects of work and the people relationships, saying directly that your most important relationship is with your boss or your immediate supervisor. Try to include the terms *respect* and *loyalty* when speaking in an organizational context and discussing a firm's products and/or services. Comment about the value you bring to any job. A sample answer follows:

> *I remember my first day of work at _____; I was faced with having to use a fax machine and an intimidating copy machine and having to learn the names and telephone extensions of all the partners! Once I got proficient with all that basic technology, the firm made a major overhaul in its approach to office technology! It was a never-ending learning curve, and I can honestly say that I never had such a good time. Since then, I have gone on to learn both the Mac and the Unix operating systems on my own.*

Keep your answer brief. Try it before your meeting. Make sure that you are impressed with the final version.

6.10   Do you think that you have top management potential?

Be realistic about your abilities, especially the higher you rise professionally.

> *I have been so fortunate to work with excellent managers; at _____, the manager delegated a lot of the reports to me because I had a knack for turning them out fast and accurately. In the past I have both worked on teams and headed up teams for long-term projects. So yes, I think I could see myself becoming more involved in operations at increasingly senior levels."*

6.11   Why did you go to law school/business school/college? Why did you attend that particular school/college?

Any question that includes the word *why* sets an adult-child tone that is the antithesis of workplace relationships. Even though you may be tempted to give a "smart" answer or perhaps a humorous one, remember your reason for meeting with the interviewer. Be ready with a firm, serious answer that demonstrates that, even as a youth with little experience, you were sure about what you wanted to do with the rest of your life.

My reason for going to college was to develop myself intellectually and to prepare for life ahead by taking the academic disciplines necessary to develop my mind. I knew then that ___ (e.g., chemistry, math, writing, or accounting) skills would always be necessary and that a(n) __ (e.g., science-based, liberal arts, or business) education would develop those skills in an organized, deliberate way.

Do not be frivolous or cute, regardless of the degree of temptation. The interviewer may possibly have positive or negative feelings about the school and may even have gone there herself—or a close family member might have been denied admission. So just give the facts.

I saw several articles written by faculty members and was impressed with their command of the subject. In addition to having a wide range of business courses, the timing of the classes allowed me to work part-time in the field that I was studying.

Remember that you are in control of what you wish to disclose and that your reason for the meeting is to continue the interview process and other selection steps so that a job offer will be given to you. For now, give the reason that makes the most sense to you and that makes you appear to be a promising candidate in the interviewer's eyes.

Although I did get a law degree, my objective was not to practice as an attorney. I felt that a legal background combined with my business degree would uniquely prepare me to assume a position in an international organization.

If you have a solid reason for a change in profession, state it succinctly. And, if you are a recent graduate or still in school (undergraduate or graduate), there is a follow-up question that is just waiting to be asked.

6.12 What was/is your best subject? Your favorite subject? Your most influential teacher? Your GPA?

When you open the door to your recent academic achievements, the interviewer may seek to explore them in great detail. If you are short on work experience, your academic experience is what you can offer—and the potential to perform in the future. Consider what classes or extracurricular activities may have specific tie-ins to the position.

Although I was an English major, I quickly got involved in campus journalism. In the beginning I was just a go-fer for the office, but it was not long before I was invited to write some small articles and progressed to being editor in my senior year.

Hopefully, the GPA question will be asked only of recent graduates, if even then. Do not panic if your GPA was less than 3.75. There may be sound reasons for it—you were more interested in learning than in the GPA, so your numbers may be lower, but you learned a lot from the tough courses with the great teachers. Other reasons for a low GPA include a heavy course load—for example, 18 credits (or more) each semester. Part-time or full-time jobs are other considerations. More include internships, study abroad, and extracurricular activities. Or consider your GPA for your major if it is better than your overall GPA. In that instance, you may mention both.

I was required to take classes in watercolor painting and figure drawing in addition to the photography classes in my major; all the photo classes earned me a 3.9 GPA, but frankly, painting and drawing were not my strong points, and I managed to get a GPA of 2.8 in those.

6.13   What made you choose to become a lawyer/chef/secretary/engineer?

Before the meeting, go through an exercise to see if you can recall your motivation for becoming a lawyer or an engineer. During the process, also determine why you chose not to go into other fields. Parents and other family members are frequently role models for our professional choices.

The important thing about this question is to demonstrate with your answer that *you were always serious about your career* and that your seriousness has carried forward to this day, so that interviewers feel that they are dealing with a prospective employee who has a solid history of professional growth and development.

I have always had a pragmatic outlook, and the field of medicine allowed me to do research without forcing me to declare my field of interest immediately. Rotating through various departments allowed me to have immediate feedback and experience to further refine my choices.

*6.14   What is our business? What do you know about our organization?

If you are unprepared for this one, you should not be sitting in this meeting in the first place. Even for courtesy interviews, be prepared by finding out whatever you can about the organization with which you will be meeting. Consider the question from a selfish point of view:

- Why might this organization be a positive move for you?
- What makes you take the time to meet with this organization rather than others?
- What value can you offer to this organization?

You owe it to yourself to learn as much as you can about any organization that you intend to visit. What you choose to share, however, really takes fine judgment on your part. If you uncover any negatives, this is not the time to share them. If you are meeting with a TV company, for example, now is not the time to speak about the appalling lack of high-quality children's programming.

Provide a concise overview of your findings that shows that you are aware of what the organization does and the size of its operations. *"XYZ bank is a tri-state bank that is committed to the retail sector. It has 42 branches, and I learned that it plans to open 7 more in the next two years."* If you show that you have some knowledge of the organization, especially if the information is not that easy to obtain, you make a good impression. Be careful not to overwhelm because the situation may become uncomfortable if you share something that the interviewer was unaware of. This same subject can be broached with other similar questions, but more specifically.

6.15 Do you use our products/services? Are you familiar with our current advertising campaign/TV or print ads? Have you visited our Web site? Do you get our newsletters?

Did you even know that the company *had* a newsletter? This should have been the easiest part of your research. If you are seeking to work for a company that sells products or services, you should know what those products or services are and where they are marketed. Without excessive detail, share a positive experience. If you have nothing good to say about what the organization sells or does, why are you there?

*6.16 What do you think our business's biggest problem is? What do you feel is our biggest advantage over our competition?

Here is an opportunity to show not only that you did your homework in preparing for this meeting, but that you have a great professional bearing and an in-depth knowledge of the industry and its other key players. Again, do not overwhelm. *Do not show up interviewers by discussing a topic in more detail than they are equipped to handle—gear your response to your audience.* Also, as far as problems are concerned, try to avoid controversy. Your interviewer may not know that you are aware of the indictments of the corporation's top three officers for price fixing unless you share it. (Remember our discussion on disclosure in Chapter 2.) Instead, select a product-related problem like the rising cost of newsprint or the decline in readership and advertising revenue if you happen to be meeting with a print media organization.

> *Organization ___ appears to have excellent demographic information. Your programs always seem to be topical and on the cutting edge, while the other networks are merely following up on the newest trends.*

*6.17 What important trends do you see in our industry?

This is a serious question that requires focus and preparation. It demands proof that you have done your homework and are prepared for an intelligent business discussion. You are meeting with the interviewer not only because you need a job, but also, regardless of your circumstances, because you have done your research and *you have real reasons for wanting to join this organization* and be a part of this specific industry. To prepare to answer this question, you need to be able to speak knowledgeably about

1. The industry
2. The issues related to the industry
3. How the organization perceives its effectiveness in dealing with the trends that the industry faces

All this is not something that takes a lifetime to learn, but it is something that requires a willingness to do research as part of the preparation for any meeting for a job. Go to the "Organization Fact Sheet" (see page 50) to determine if you have enough information to speak intelligently about the industry. Of particular importance is how you can see yourself making a positive difference to the organization in the future.

> *Clearly the biggest trend is the move to online communication. Interactive "magazines" may be the wave of the future, and, with my journalism background combined with my HTML experience, I am really excited about how I will help change the future of the publishing industry.*

HOW TO BE A LIFELONG LEARNER

❏ In your own eyes, **see yourself as a perennial student**. Try to develop an open mind and become a student of human nature.

❏ **Be aware** of what is happening in your industry and in the economy.

❏ **Maintain professional relationships**, particularly if you are currently unemployed. Attend seminars and workshops whenever possible.

❏ **Volunteer**, on a limited basis, for enterprises like Junior Achievement or as a mentor where you can use your skills and talents. Seek a position in a local college to teach your subject matter in your "off hours."

❏ Think of this **job search as a chance to learn**: to learn about yourself, to learn about other organizations, and to learn about others.

❏ **You never know what you might learn through this research.** You may discover further leads that you never considered, job opportunities that you might have missed, or information that might prove helpful in subsequent interviews.

❏ **Commit** to registering for at least one conference, seminar, course (online or traditional), or Webinar every six months.

7

WHAT HAVE YOU DONE?

(AND WHAT CAN YOU DO FOR US?)

*A*re you a one-trick pony? Do you have what is needed? Is your past a predic-tor of your future with us? How can we be sure that we are hiring the right person? Can you do what you say you can? Did you do what you say you have done?

Experience questions are the most important to deal with for three reasons:

1. *Experience questions require applicants to review what they have previously done in their professional lives.* This exercise provides an opportunity for re-call and analysis, something that all people who are serious about their work should do periodically. If you do not go through this exercise, then a lot of what you have done in the past will be lost, and you could possibly repeat your mistakes, because we all tend to forget situations and, most important, their outcomes as time passes unless we make a conscious effort to recall them periodically.

2. *Your past and current experiences can determine whether the interview pro-cess goes forward.* These questions may be framed as behavioral questions and are frequently the benchmark that the interviewer uses to make the decision to continue the interview process, and ultimately to make the hire/don't hire decision.

3. *These questions are a great opportunity for you to shine, for who is a better expert on you than you yourself are?* It would be folly for you not to be fully prepared for questions regarding your past experience and thus lose a great opportunity to sell yourself. Just as manufacturers package their products in attractive boxes and develop marketing campaigns to tout their products' latest advantages, you must create a sales campaign for yourself. What are your best points? How can you add value to the organization? To retain in-terviewers' interest, you must present a positive image from the first moment

you meet them, and the more details you are able to provide from your past work experiences, the more likely you are to make the sale.

Experience questions can take various forms:

Describe your last job.

Tell me about your last boss/team/employer.

Tell me about a time when . . .

What would you do if . . .?

What was your biggest mistake? Your proudest moment? Your biggest surprise about your last job?

Putting Your Best Foot Forward

There are a lot of emotions swirling around in every interview. The traits given here are the personal characteristics that need to be displayed throughout every interview, but especially in responses to questions regarding one's experience.

TRAITS TO DEMONSTRATE IN RESPONSES TO EXPERIENCE QUESTIONS

❏ **Preparation.** You are taking the interview process seriously.

❏ **Enthusiasm.** You are excited by the work that you have already done and are looking forward to the future.

❏ **Communication effectiveness.** You are able to speak cogently and appear to be a savvy person who can discuss your work in an interesting and intelligent manner.

❏ **Focus.** The main topic of an interview should be your skills and your professional experience.

❏ **Subject matter expert.** You are *the expert* on what you have been doing at work.

❏ **Passion.** It is really helpful if you can demonstrate the excitement that you feel for both the work you do and the work you would do in the new job.

❏ **A sense of urgency.** The more you convey the importance that you feel for what you do, the more you will communicate a need that you had to meet that drove you to take action. The interviewer will hope that that same sense of urgency will be displayed in the organization that is interviewing you, if you are hired.

Preinterview Preparation

All the interviewer may know about you is what is on your résumé and in your cover letter. In the interview itself, he will seek insights into and details of your professional experience, including your relationships with superiors and subordinates; information regarding your experiences with teams, projects, and tasks (both positive and negative); and other information regarding your work experience.

Preinterview preparation is time well spent because it offers you an opportunity to consider your job from another (and frequently missed) vantage point. *Three hours of preparation, including research on the organization and the industry, appears to be a reasonable amount of time to invest for each interview.* A first step is to take a copy of your most recent résumé and come up with all the details and salient points of your professional history that are not included in the résumé itself, but that you should have literally "at the tip of your tongue" for your interview. Using the "Experience Worksheet" (see below), provide all the details (who, what, when, where, and why) for your current or most recent job and for all the jobs listed on your résumé. Do not omit any military service or volunteer experience; if you are asked to complete a job application, this information will be useful to have with you.

EXPERIENCE WORKSHEET

Provide details for each job listed on your résumé, starting with the current or most recent.

Employer: _____

Address: _____

Telephone number: _____

Supervisor's name: _____

Supervisor's telephone number:_____

Supervisor's e-mail: _____

Date started: _____

Last day of work: _____

Starting salary: _____

Current/ending salary: _____

Starting position: _____

Current/ending position: _____

Starting title: _____

EXPERIENCE WORKSHEET *(Continued)*

How did you get this job? _____

_____

Describe your most recent duties: _____

_____

Describe your work group: _____

On what basis was your work evaluated? _____

Who evaluated your work? _____

How often? _____

What evaluation did you last receive? _____

How many hours did you usually work each week? _____

Overtime? _____

How often? _____

Why? _____

What did you like best about this job? _____

_____

What did you like least? _____

_____

What were your greatest accomplishments? _____

_____

What skills did you use? _____

_____

What were your major responsibilities? _____

_____

Promotions/awards/honors? _____

_____

Why did you leave this position? _____

Continue your preparation for these questions by looking at critical incidents that were a part of your job during the past three months or the last three months that you were there, if you have been out awhile. The reason for taking the last three months is that when you start by considering your most recent experience, this first exercise makes it easier for you to recall earlier incidents (six months or a year earlier).

Critical incidents are those that are outside of the customary and ordinary process of doing business under usual or ordinary circumstances. They should be the most exciting part of any job because they represent a challenge. The situations may require high risk but also offer greater reward. Use the "Critical Incidents Worksheet" (see below) to perform this exercise. Do not confine your review to those incidents where things were all in your favor, but include times when problems ensued or when your work was criticized. What did you learn from these "mistakes"?

CRITICAL INCIDENTS WORKSHEET

List critical incidents from each of your past jobs and what skills and/or achievements were involved.

SITUATION—describe an incident that resulted in your bringing about a positive outcome	TASK—identify activities that were a part of that process	ACTION—disclose the steps that you took	RESULT—relate the result and compare the actual to the planned/anticipated result

A popular technique called the "STAR method" may help you present your success stories in a very organized, easy-to-remember way. You should approach these answers by first describing the Situation. Next, identify the Tasks that you performed in that situation. The third step is to name the Actions that you took to deal with the situation effectively. Finally, you should mention the *Result* that occurred.

> *While I was working as the human resources rep for the Case Management unit, the head of the unit shared her frustration with the amount of time that the case managers had to spend completing reports that included detailed notes about visits with clients. She also noted that the case managers received little training in what should be included in these visit reports. She suggested that a task force be formed to design a template that would clearly display the information sought. Case managers were also encouraged to use appropriate phrases taken from a menu of terms. I worked with the group to iron out any wrinkles, which included installing the template and the menu of phrases. The template has since been made the standard form. The result was that reimbursements are now received earlier, since it takes the case managers less time to complete the forms, allowing them to spend more time where they want to be—with their clients.*

Parameters of the Job You Are Interviewing For

What do you feel are the key requirements for the position? You can look back at your work history to see what you have *done*, but what might you be required *to do* in the new job? Those are the topics that are most likely to be explored in the interview.

List the job's requirements and environment as you understand them in the "Job Opening Outline" (see page 105) prior to the interview; you can add the missing elements to your list of questions to ask at the interview if they are not provided in the course of your discussion. Complete one of these outlines prior to each scheduled interview. For example, in "Technical Requirements," list any software programs required (either as stated in the advertised job opening or from your research); in "Skills/Experience," budgeting or supervising staff or customer service; in "Environment," would you expect to work as part of a team or a group, or be on a one-to-one basis with clients?

JOB OPENING OUTLINE

Position: _____

Organization _____

Job title: _____ Salary offered: _____

Technical requirements: _____

_____

Skills/experience: _____

_____

Environment: _____

_____

_____

*7.1 Describe your current/last work group. What is/What was it like working with your current/last work group?

This is an open-ended question designed to determine what characteristics the work group has that you feel are important enough to disclose. Briefly mention the composition of the work group. Use major demographic categories—education level, gender, other EEO categories (marital status, race, national origin, age, or religion), or whatever is appropriate to assist the interviewer in determining the kind of group you have experience working with. (Refer to page 187 for a related question asked in a more blatant way.) The more relevant the details, the more helpful your description will be. Don't stop here. Go on to characterize the group in terms of the work situation—tight-knit, strong work ethic, good-natured but serious about work—so that the interviewer is able to complete the picture and to compare it to the one you would be dealing with if a job were offered to you.

Avoid gossip or catty details. Applicants should avoid using the terms *girls, boys, guys,* and *gals* entirely. *Colleagues, associates, team members,* or *the other men and women* are terms that are much more professional and appropriate.

Last year two departments were combined, and we all found ourselves needing to reinvent how we met production quotas. A few of us from each group got together and literally drew up a new program and presented it both to our supervisor and the entire group. There was some give and take ironing out the final proposal, but it was a process that resulted in a more efficient division.

7.2 Let me describe the work group you would be joining if we offered you the position. How would you fit in? In this position, how would you see your role as team member/builder?

The employer is asking you to consider the circumstances and the environment of the workplace if the job is offered to you, and also offering you insight into the work group. Is it as you thought it would be? You want to address this question whether or not the interviewer asks it; in fact, you should be asking it of yourself. Can you see yourself working here, in this situation?

Use terms to describe your prior roles in the work group: *facilitator, leader, synthesizer, enabler, consensus builder*, and/or *supporter*. Use whatever term is an accurate, brief description of the role you played as a member of the team and how you would see yourself fitting in at the organization where you are interviewing.

An aspect of this question that should not be overlooked is that the answer requires you to have a realistic understanding of the position and the work group. An example of a strong but brief answer is

> *Since I have had experience in my last position starting a(n) ___ department, being able to attend to details as well as to consider the human element gives me resources to draw upon in expanding the __ area here.*

7.3 What would be your ideal work group? Size and type?

Be honest with yourself in your preparation for the interview. Be ready to answer this question, but remember that the interviewer's reason for asking it is to determine whether you are compatible with the work group that you would be joining if a job offer were extended. There are two approaches to this question.

1. If the employer has already shared her perceptions of the major characteristics of the work group with you, then you need to determine which of those elements are most compatible with yours. By identifying them, you are striving to demonstrate that there is a fit.
2. If the interviewer has not disclosed any characteristics of the work group, take a positive approach, and if it is perceived to be slightly idealized, that is fine. Here is an example.

> *My ideal work group would be one in which there is an infusion of a strong work ethic throughout the group. Additionally, each of the participants would have a real commitment to the work and to a high-quality product and a respect for one another and for the organization that*

they are a part of. The group would be so effective in playing to the team members' strengths and supporting any weaknesses that it would actually perform with very little guidance and direction. If a problem were to arise, it would be addressed and solved by the group itself.

or

I have worked with groups that required a lot of training to adapt to new procedures as well as the group I am working with now, all of whose members are highly seasoned employees that require little supervision. I have to admit that I enjoyed both ends of the spectrum.

Unless you really have strong reasons to back up your opinion, don't paint yourself into a corner.

I worked in a large department at _____, and I am currently part of a five-person team. The responsibilities and projects differ, so I feel that the number of people involved is not the sole criterion; the task, the time frame, and the resources available are all part of the picture.

*7.4   How would you define a conducive work environment?

In addition to a description of the work group, expand your answer to include the following:

A supervisor who is a good communicator and enhances the productivity of the work group by sharing responsibility for output level and quality with each of the team members. He or she also realizes the importance of balancing task requirements with relationships. And last, an organization that values its employees.

7.5   What do you feel would be a difficult work environment? Have you ever had to deal with a difficult work environment? What happened?

The most difficult work environment I have had to deal with was the one I just came out of. We all knew that the company was in financial trouble, and there had been waves of layoffs. There was a fair amount of stress, since fewer people had to cover more of the work as a result of this cost cutting. Overall, I think we pulled together as long as we could, trying to make the situation work and hoping that someone would buy the company. It did not happen, and we were all let go.

7.6 Have you ever had to fire someone? Describe the circumstances and how you handled the situation.

Expect this question whenever you have disclosed on your résumé and/or at your interview that you have managerial experience. Firing employees goes with the territory. If you have not fired anyone, the thinking is (and it is valid) that you have not had a complete management experience. (This alone doesn't make you a complete manager, but it is an action without which it is difficult to demonstrate in-depth management experience.)

If you have never fired an employee, say so. If you were involved, regardless of the level, but you were not the decision maker, condition your response with the fact that you were part of the process and leave it at that.

The easiest answer is an affirmative one with no conditions or hedging. If you have done it, say so and stop. Terminating someone is one of the most difficult issues that a manager has to deal with for several reasons. If the termination is due to a staff restructuring or downsizing, you severed someone's employment because the position was eliminated, not because of the person's performance. *Expressing sympathy with those whose jobs were lost and acknowledging the psychological and economic concerns show that you do not take these tasks lightly.*

As ___ manager, I was often responsible for informing employees on my staff that, in line with the company's plan to curtail operations, a few of their positions were being eliminated. More often than not, the handwriting was already on the wall, but in a few cases the employee was genuinely shocked. Fortunately, a generous severance package and outplacement counseling were being offered, but I found that very little could be done to soften the blow.

Since I was in charge of the unit, I was responsible for the annual review of staff members. Several times I had to put employees on warnings for poor performance and then follow up with termination. In one case, I was able to get the employee transferred to another area that was more suited to her skills.

You might add,

I usually do not transfer problems, but this situation was just a mismatch and I really felt that the employee was an asset to the company, so I went to bat for her, and it really worked out, since she is still there after five years.

*Our organization had a centralized human resources/personnel func-
tion, and, although we recommended termination, they implemented the
decision. Recommending termination was never an easy task.*

**7.7   Have you ever had to hire someone? For what types of positions/sal-
ary levels? What do you look for when you hire someone?**

Yes, regularly for ____ positions in our ____ department.

If you feel that you have not actually had to hire someone, be careful before saying no to this question. Were you involved in the hiring process, but are you now
tempted to say no because you feel that you were not the final decision maker?

Remember also to consider circumstances when you were not an employee
(e.g., as a volunteer in a not-for-profit organization or in a situation when you
had to serve as a home-care provider). In this situation, you may have had the
opportunity to hire one or more individuals, but you may not recall the situation
because it occurred outside the workplace. Even though it occurred outside the
workplace, the interviewer may relate to it.

This question demonstrates the seriousness of the person who is meeting
with you. Expect the question to be raised in every situation where you will be
expected to be involved in the hiring process. This is certainly true for applicants
who are taking positions in the recruiting and selection (often called "staffing" or
"employment") area of human resources, as well as for others with hiring responsibility, usually at manager level or above.

The characteristics that are frequently sought today, along with experience,
include a strong work ethic, loyalty, knowledge, dedication, passion, and a sense
of urgency. Another way to break it down is by starting with an overview statement:

*At _____ Company, they had a very family-oriented viewpoint, and in
addition to skills and experience requirements, they really felt it was
extremely important that the hire fit into the company. Consequently,
there often were group interviews of prospective management hires,
and as head of a department, I was usually involved.*

There may be a hidden agenda at work: defining your own hire. Are you
strong on "will do," but do not have much experience to back you up? Stress
that you look for potential, that you are hiring for today and for the future. If you
have a varied background and are a chameleon in the workplace, say that you
value "fit" because the interpersonal element is so important. This assumes that
the basic job requirements ("can do") have been met. With time and more rec-

ognition for the complexity of any job, it is difficult to conceive of any recruiting and selection interview that does not attempt to identify the "will do" and "fit" categories in every candidate. To avoid questioning on these issues makes any hire more of a risk.

7.8 What interview questions did you ask that persuaded you to hire or not? How did your hire(s) work out?

This is not a chance to teach someone how to interview; as much as possible, describe a situation similar to the one that you are now in.

Much as this interview has done so far, I would discuss prior responsibilities as well as technical expertise. Supervisory duties were not part of the job, but ability to work on long-term projects was, so that was a key element. Other than one hire whose spouse had to suddenly relocate, everyone I hired is still with the company.

INGREDIENTS FOR A SUCCESSFUL HIRE

❑ **"Can do."** The job candidate has the ability to do the job. She has done the job in the past and can show specifics in her work history where the skills and requirements needed here have been utilized.

❑ **"Will do."** This measures the job candidate's effectiveness potential. He demonstrates enthusiasm and understanding of the company, the job, and the industry. He can do what we need here.

❑ **"Fit."** The job candidate comes from an industry, organization, or work group similar to ours, and has insight into our priorities and our environment. She can be successful here.

7.9 Have you ever had to motivate or build team spirit among coworkers? Describe why this happened.

Consider this an opportunity to obtain information about the organization and the work group that you are going to be working with if an offer is extended. First, you need to answer the question. You should be prepared for this question because of your detailed review of your work experiences before this meeting. Disclose the best situation that you were ever involved with, preferably as an employee, but consider any team situation (including sports or community groups). Describe the circumstances briefly to show that you have leadership and take-charge ability (as well as the skill to analyze situations to determine when "soft" leadership skills and intuition are required). Once you have answered the question, add without pausing, *"Tell me if that same skill will be required here."* Wait for the response without another word, regardless of the length of time before the interviewer replies. The longer the silence, the more important the answer is.

*7.10 Have you ever worked for, or with, a difficult person?

Do not get philosophical about all the various shades of meaning of the word *difficult*, but realize that once you start to answer, you have essentially assumed that the other person was "difficult" while you were not. You can avoid the dilemma by starting with, *"If by difficult you mean a person who _____, then, yes, I have."* Examples may include a person who

- Never allowed a typographical error.
- Set impossible deadlines all the time.
- Was totally against trying new methods.
- Trusted no one to take responsibility for anything.
- Would never delegate.
- Would never give credit, yet took all the credit regardless of the circumstances.
- Never admitted to making even a minor mistake.

When you answer, make sure that the difficulty is obvious and simple to describe, as well as likely to generate agreement from the interviewer. Be on the lookout for gray areas that may cause confusion. One possibility is a "clean desk" (or "messy desk") person unless you are fairly certain that you and the interviewer are on the same page of the issue you introduce. Tread carefully. The office where the interview is taking place may not be her office.

7.11 How many of your bosses were male? Female? Were most of your coworkers male or female (or in other EEO categories)?

You should have addressed this question in your review of your experience. Usually it is asked of an applicant who possesses an opposite characteristic (that is, a woman might be asked how many of her bosses and coworkers were men). Interviewers ask the question if they feel the need to determine whether you have had any experience in that kind of environment. If you have, be direct and positive: *"I have had three female bosses [coworkers], and each was a very positive experience, as you will see when you check my references."*

If you have not had varied experiences, say so, but try to qualify it.

Although I have not had the opportunity to work for a female supervisor directly, I have dealt with women in supervisory capacities in meetings and with clients.

All of the supervisors in my department are men, but I have had many professional dealings with women in other departments and in coordinating projects. I feel that a variety of factors are key to any supervisor/subordinate relationship, but a primary one is the work ethic, and therefore I am confident that this will not be a problem.

7.12 How much time on your current/last job is/was spent working alone? Which do you prefer—working alone or with a group?

The purpose of this question is to further the interviewer's understanding of your prior/current work environment. Ideally, look for balance between doing your own work alone and in the presence of others, mirroring what you feel will be the situation in the new job. By showing balance, you eliminate the opportunity for the interviewer to dismiss your application because the job available is the opposite of the situation that you describe. Always remember that no matter how much you want the job offer, you will have to do the job, so don't paint yourself into a situation where you will not feel comfortable or be effective. If you hate being out on your own but thrive in a group atmosphere (review your "My Ideal Job" questionnaire on page 42), be honest in your answers, as the follow-up may be the next question.

State simply that either is an effective environment for you unless you feel strongly that one works for you and the other doesn't. In that case, state it directly and wait for the interviewer's response. If the situation is the opposite of your strong preference, it may be a deal breaker. But if you are sure that it is, then do not backtrack, thereby allowing the interviewer to perceive you as weak.

I know that I do not need close supervision and am a self-starter, but I have had such great team experiences leading motivated groups that I would love to repeat that.

7.13 How often did you meet with your supervisor? For what purpose?

This direct question is an opportunity for interviewers to determine what supervisory style you have been working under. It allows them to determine the extent of your autonomy.

We met at the start of each day to determine our priorities and identify what was to be accomplished during that shift.

We have established a routine of meeting first thing Monday morning and setting our priorities for the week. I e-mail a progress report early Friday, which we then review over the telephone to see what needs tweaking before the week ends.

7.14   In your current/past position, how important is/was communication and dealing with others? In your current/past position, what role does/did communication play?

Communication is being regarded as increasingly important in every organization. The interviewer is asking you to show your regard for it as well. Any answer with *"not very important"* anywhere in it is perceived as weak, and you with it. Regardless of the position, its level, the organization, the industry, or the sector, you need to be convinced of the importance of communication in every position.

Communication was very important in my last position because to complete our work successfully, we needed to learn of any changes from the ___ department as quickly as they occurred, or else errors would result.

7.15   What form of communication do you prefer? Which do you feel is most effective?

Think about the ideal communication environment before you respond. "What is the easiest form of communication?" is the way the question would probably be phrased if it were being asked in a college communications course. Consider the choices: verbal and nonverbal communication. Of the two, obviously verbal communication is less likely to cause misunderstanding.

With regard to verbal communication, there are two types: oral (in the workplace, the two major categories are face-to-face and telephone) and written. Rank them from easiest to most difficult. If you follow the same order as written in the preceding sentence, you agree with everyone that, unless there are mitigating circumstances (e.g., two people who become incensed anytime they meet), face-to-face communication is the most effective. It is the most direct, and it allows the participants to be sensitive to the nonverbal messages and nuances.

Any reply that states that written communication is the form you prefer or the most effective raises concern with most interviewers. The best interviewers probe to learn more about the answer. Others consider the answer as coming from a person for whom protocol and procedure take precedence over effective communication.

I have always found that direct conversations have been the most effective, with occasional written follow-ups.

7.16 Do you instant message? Do you Twitter? Do you like to use e-mails? Do you have a BlackBerry or iPhone?

This could be an inquiry into how in touch you are with the newest technology, or it could be concerned with how much time you might waste in keeping up with your social networking; it also may relate to the company's need to be in touch with its employees 24/7. Consider the source of the question: is it a high-tech company or not?

> At _____, we used in-house e-mails to keep everyone up to date on a variety of projects in between departmental meetings, and we were issued iPhones/ BlackBerrys to keep in touch with tech support and clients. The best was a shared departmental calendar that we all posted our appointments on.

*7.17 Describe how your last/current job related to the overall goals of your department and organization. What impact did it have on the company's profit or loss?

All employees, regardless of level, should be aware of the roles that their positions play in achieving the goals of the department and how these departmental goals relate to the goals of the organization, particularly in this vulnerable economy. This relates directly to "value added"—what value do you add to the organization? This should be true for the not-for-profit and the public sector, as well as the private sector.

> Since I was the budget officer, every department relied on my monthly reports to analyze whether it was meeting or exceeding projections. In turn, I relied on the various departments' submitting accurate production reports on a timely basis. It became a real team effort because there was a profit-sharing incentive in place, so everyone wanted to control expenses and increase production.

> In the shipping department, we had a direct impact on costs, so it was imperative that goods be moved quickly and accurately; we maintained a "How many did we ship today?" chart to cheer us on.

7.18 Did you bring work home? Did you work from home? Did you take all the vacation/time off that you were entitled to? What is your attitude toward lunch? What about eating at one's desk?

In other words, are you a dedicated worker or a workaholic? Do you socialize with fellow workers during lunch breaks, or are you a loner? If needed, can you work late, take work home, or, if you are ill, work from home? This question can be taken two ways—one, to see how committed you are to your career, and two, to send warning signals that this job might be 24/7!

I never have a problem stepping up if the job needs extra effort or hours. Do you envision any situations that would require extensive extra hours?

When we had business to conduct with Tokyo, I would make myself available at 9 p.m. because of the time differences. If no conference call was planned, I would try to leave at a reasonable time each day. What will be expected of me here?

*7.19 Do/Did you work on major projects in your current/most recent job? Tell me about a project in your current/last job that you really got excited about. What were/are the most important projects that you completed on your last/current job?

Again, regardless of your job level, use your "Experience Worksheet" (pages 101–102) and your "Critical Incidents Worksheet" (page 103) prior to your interviews to determine the aspects of your position that are project-oriented (as opposed to process-oriented or operational). If you feel that none of your projects would qualify as "major," in the interviewer's perception, then preface your remarks with that comment: *"I don't think any of the projects that I have participated in will qualify as 'major.' Nonetheless, let me tell you about one that was essential to . . . ."*

If you are at a loss and cannot think of any project at all in your current job, think about your outside and family activities. Be careful not to overlook relocations, long-term-care considerations, selecting a college, planning a wedding (or even a vacation!), preparing for a mortgage closing, or providing leadership for an event. (There are people all over the country who take responsibility for chairing fund-raising events that are as large and complex as the projects of all but the largest organizations. Don't forget to mention one that you took responsibility for.)

Until very recently, projects were not given the status and consideration in the workplace that they warrant. Frequently, being placed on a special project was a euphemism for being shown the door. The project skills that one develops are an essential part of the baggage that professionals bring with them to the workplace, and the skills required to bring a project to a successful completion are certainly traits to be recognized and valued. With all the reorganizing that is taking place in an ongoing way in organizations in every industry and sector throughout the United States, those who are able to be effective in project assignments bring with them a package of skills that is going to be a real asset in the organization's efforts to maximize its effectiveness.

7.20   How do you plan and organize for a major long-range project?

Here, use your planning and organizing experience as a reference point to discuss the question in the most effective manner. It does not matter whether the project you are discussing was inside or outside work; what is important is that you demonstrate quickly and briefly that you know how to plan and organize for a major long-range project. This is an opportunity for a tag question. At the end of your answer, be sure to add (if you feel comfortable doing so), *"Will there be opportunities for me to use these skills in the position we are discussing?"* This tag-on gets you more details on the scope and nature of the position. This is a good time to use the *"STAR* method" (see page 103) and tell a *brief* story about a project from conception to completion, showing how you worked.

Another version of this question or a follow-up seeking more details could be: "Tell me about a long-range project that you planned and organized; what was the outcome?"

7.21   How many projects can you handle at one time?

You need to balance and hedge. You do not want to portray yourself as a slave who takes on an increasing number of projects and never says no, but you want to demonstrate that you devour work and love the opportunity to be of assistance. A careful answer starts with a review of your own experience to determine what that experience has been.

I have had overlap in projects in the past that were completed on schedule because I had the resources, both personnel and materials, that I needed to do so.

Part of my credibility is my practice of never accepting more than I anticipate with reasonable certainty that I will be able to complete effectively and on schedule. If situations or priorities change, I sit down with management and restructure my schedule, bringing my concerns to management as quickly as I identify them, so that there is little likelihood of any surprises—especially negative ones—surfacing.

7.22   What activities did/do you perform in your last/current position, and what was/is the approximate time devoted to these activities?

Consider this a request for a mini job description. When an approximate amount of time is requested, percentages work effectively. If the job is directly tied to time of day and the work is fairly consistent on a daily basis, then choose a time format.

I usually reserved the first part of the morning for going through mail and reports, and returning telephone calls. Late mornings I would visit the manufacturing floor, touching base with the various section heads. If any problems had arisen, this would permit me to schedule a meeting after lunch to discuss the situation in detail with the appropriate divisions. Afternoons were divided between telephone follow-ups with clients and suppliers, keeping appointments, and weekly meetings with senior management.

For percentage:

Approximately 30 percent of my day was spent calling vendors to ensure that delivery dates continued to be firm. Another 30 percent was spent researching new product possibilities. About 15 percent was for correspondence, and 5 percent was for our intern. The last 20 percent was reserved for meetings inside and outside the organization.

Notice that no percentage is less than 5 percent and that the total comes to 100 percent.

7.23 What was/is your workload like on your last/current job?

Now is not the time to complain about how unreasonable your supervisors were at your last place of employment (even if that is the reason that you left/are leaving). If the workload was heavy, say so and provide a few brief details, quantifying the situation if possible, to support your opinion. Relate the details, if possible, to the open position that you are interviewing for:

As in your organization, when we approached the publication date, work escalated, and overtime was often required. There was a definite ebb and flow to the workload, with some months, like our double holiday issue, being especially frantic, coming at that time of year. The key to my being able to handle the extra work was expecting it to come because it always did.

*7.24 What were/are your most important decisions on your last/current job?

Take a matter-of-fact tone and identify the aspects of your job that gave you the opportunity to make meaningful decisions. The level of the position dictates the weight of the decisions. It is perfectly acceptable (in fact, it may be encouraged) to identify the opportunity to make decisions that were slightly beyond the expected scope of your position, but it is folly to identify decisions that were clearly below your station as important. A vice president may readily mention a $2 million credit authority level, and an assembly-line worker may mention the authority to shut down the line. However, an administrative assistant who takes credit for an increase in sales or a department manager who boasts about the annual picnic or the quarterly fire drill will not be regarded favorably by the interviewer.

7.25 In what ways has your current/last job prepared you to take on greater responsibility?

By reviewing the experiences that you had during your stay in your last job, you may now well reflect on what your next job should be. The more the situation is similar (if not identical) to the position you are interviewing for, the more the interviewer will consider the "fit."

When my immediate supervisor was called away for jury duty, it took even longer than anticipated; he was sequestered for several weeks! During his absence, I was responsible for running the division, and I enjoyed it immensely. Deadlines and production adhered to schedule.

7.26 Describe a situation when you had to make a quick "seat of the pants" decision. What choices did you think you had, and what was the outcome?

Preferably you should see this as an opportunity to describe a situation at work, although, if you cannot think of one at work, take it from your personal experiences. The goal of this question is to determine the applicant's ability to make a reasonable decision quickly when there is no one to turn to. Be careful to show yourself not as someone who makes the decision to release a nuclear bomb, but as someone who is not afraid to make a decision if some risk is involved and who recognizes when more risk is involved in making no decision at all.

When I was serving as a lifeguard, once the rain started, I ordered the pool abandoned even though there was no lightning, because two days before, in another pool nearby, a child had been struck by lightning under the same circumstances.

*7.27 How were you evaluated on your last/current job? Give an example of a situation when you received constructive feedback.

Clarify whether you are being asked about the method of evaluation or about the evaluation you received. (Actually, without knowing how the evaluation was generated, the final result is a bit worthless, so if all the interviewer is interested in is the grade, how perceptive is she?) Be brief and honest. Do not elaborate on an issue that you may be particularly sensitive to.

We were on an MBO [management by objectives] system, and we had our goals reviewed and updated every quarter.

It is hard to say because I was there three years and never got a review.

I was fortunate because I was aware of the fact that I should get periodic feedback. So during one of our one-on-one weekly meetings, I asked my supervisor to tell me the strong and weak elements of my performance from the preceding week. He seemed to like my approach, and I certainly appreciated his frank and timely comments.

7.28   Have you been involved in/responsible for performance reviews of others? Describe the process.

Once I was promoted to supervisor, I was responsible for the annual review of the five staff members in my department. Since I was given detailed feedback during my performance reviews, this was great preparation for my being in a position to provide constructive criticism and feedback to my staff.

7.29   What are some things that you find difficult to do? Why?

Either identify job elements that you perceive as being tedious and of minor importance to the interviewer or discuss something regarding your performance that you are taking action to improve. This is a good opportunity to use someone else's observations, to paraphrase someone else if you can.

One of my coworkers said the other day: "You have all those index cards on your desk. What do you do with them?" I have a habit of backing up all my sales notes on cards, such as a certain client's kids' names or the fact that he is vegan. I keep postponing putting these comments into my computer files for fear of losing them.

With everything else going on, I sometimes find it difficult to find the time to file; knowing this, I usually plan on coming in a bit early one day a week and just catching up.

Keeping up with paperwork is sometimes difficult, if not impossible, because new orders are coming in all the time. I have recommended that we change over to a computerized order-tracking system, but so far, nothing has happened.

Or take a positive twist and make it a positive "problem."

Because service is such an important hallmark of our approach to internal as well as external customers, I find it difficult to say no, even when the issue that is being raised is not directly related to what we do, when I know that I can be of service, even it if is only to contact the person who can solve the problem.

I get so involved that it is tough to stop at the end of the day.

7.30 How do you remain effective when you are faced with difficult tasks or with things that you do not like to do?

Consider your "Experience Worksheet" (see pages 101–102) to review which aspects of your most recent position you enjoy doing and which you do not. Consider your responsibilities also in terms of difficult versus easy tasks. People in the organizing and time management industry all encourage you to complete the most difficult and least liked tasks before you complete any others (since if you put off the most difficult tasks, chances are that you will run out of time before you are able to deal with them).

7.31 How does your current or prior organization compare with us (the organization that you are interviewing with)?

If you do not know, it is reasonable for you to ask as long as the interviewer brought up the subject. Point out any positive parallels.

At the two foreign banks where I worked, I became very flexible about frequent changes in senior management. I found that one key to my success was to remain nonpolitical and show loyalty to the company. As your business is part of an international corporation, I imagine that the turnover may be quite similar.

7.32 Have you ever changed the nature of your job? How?

With so much reorganization taking place in the workplace, in addition to the popularity of self-directed work teams, it is quite possible that you have had the opportunity to participate in the reorganization of your own job. If you have, say so, and describe the details briefly. Any positive answer, either in your professional or your personal life, shows your creativity and problem-solving ability.

In an attempt to streamline operations, two offices were combined, and our location was the one eliminated. There were some staff reductions and reassignments, and we all had to work out new schedules, determine whom to report to, and reevaluate our workloads, and I ended up handling more international clients than I had before. Despite the fact that it happened very fast, it did go smoothly, and we did not lose a single customer.

7.33 **Have you ever had to make an unpopular decision or announcement? Describe it and tell me how you handled it.**

A review of your "Experience Worksheet" (see pages 101–102) or your "Critical Incidents Worksheet" (see page 103) may identify a time when you had to make an unpopular decision. Now is the time to share it with your interviewer. Do not consider only major situations. Even if as a clerk, you needed to bring a matter to the attention of your supervisor, risking the wrath of your coworkers, now is the time to mention it. Employers look for loyalty to the organization and to your supervisors, combined with real experience with tough situations.

When I first arrived to assume my role as HR generalist for the facility, the clinical staff had long been accustomed to big overtime payments for backing up each other with unplanned absences. It seemed that management preferred doing nothing about this, since coverage was always maintained. The union, too, felt that its members were happy about the arrangement, so if management did not mind the payroll expense, it was fine with the employees working double shifts. The problem was that the organization could no longer afford the additional expense. So instead of confronting the issue head-on, I convinced management to enforce time and attendance policies to eliminate unscheduled absences. The union even agreed with the strict policy as long as it was universally enforced. The result was a more effective organization, with tighter controls and a boost in morale among those clinical staff members who had always resented the fact that their colleagues were exploiting a situation for their own financial gain.

*7.34 **In your current/past position, how many levels of management do/did you have to communicate with? On what issues and levels do/did you deal with management?**

The interviewer is trying to determine the range of your contacts in your last position. In an effort to give substance to your answer, and also as a reality check, provide the functional and corporate titles (never the names) of those you communicated with and briefly describe the purpose and extent of the contact.

In addition to the ongoing contact with the vice president for manufacturing and the district sales manager, I had to deal with the relocation officer for a major move that our department was going through and see the CFO monthly for budget variances.

7.35 In your current/past position, what problems did you identify that had previously been overlooked? What actions did you take or recommend?

Here is a chance for you to shine by being prepared. The interviewer is trying to determine your ability to see beyond the confines of the day-to-day activities of your position and significantly improve the position's output and effectiveness. A major reason for bringing someone in from the outside to fill a position is to get a fresh look at the situation and bring in new ideas. You want the interviewer to think "can do" and "will do," and raise the hope that you have new creative and practical solutions in your repertoire.

7.36 What do you think is the most difficult aspect of being a manager/ executive?

"Having to give bad news" is as succinct and to the point as one can get. This is a brief, valid answer that begs the serious interviewer to ask you for more. A superficial interviewer does not pursue this issue with additional questions to flesh out your thought-provoking response and to determine whether there is substance and a demonstration of in-depth experience behind the answer. This response addresses how a manager reacts to difficult situations.

A second response demonstrates that the manager is ready to take control and provide leadership from the start: *"Getting the group of people that you have inherited to respond quickly and effectively to your authority."*

Motivating people and finding (as well as building) the team are additional areas to explore in developing an effective approach to this question. Both certainly demonstrate to the interviewer the depth of your experience and your ability to be trusted with the responsibility for managing others.

7.37 What do you think makes this position different from your last/current position?

Look for a positive aspect that distinguishes the two. If that point demonstrates that you will be a strong employee, then you are answering the question successfully.

The work group seems more cohesive; have the same members worked together long?

The management appears more supportive.

With your recent reorganization, I feel that the challenges may be greater. I have been through two other reorganizations, and I know how much energy is needed to work everything out.

7.38 What do you wish you had accomplished at your last/current position that you were unable to accomplish?

A promotion, a new assignment, and a relocation all have to do with your positioning. Another approach is to target specific changes in the process: *"The introduction of new technology, a turnaround time of less than 20 minutes, lower turnover."* These are all perfectly acceptable alternatives because they again allow the interviewer to think, "can do—will do."

7.39 What kinds of decisions are most difficult for you?

Identify those that involve either a human relations issue or a lower or subordinate level. Concentrate on those dealing with tough choices:

Do I give another chance to the person who has just broken the machinery for the third time?

Do I vote to close the plant because productivity has been falling for the last three quarters and one of four plants must be closed?

7.40 When you have to make a difficult decision, where do you seek guidance?

No matter where I have worked, I have always found more experienced staff members who seem to have "seen it all" and have a wealth of knowledge that they are willing to share. I am glad to bounce ideas off of others when I need some guidance. While seeking advice, though, I always remember that I am ultimately responsible for the decision.

*7.41 What makes you think that you could handle a position that requires so many diverse talents and persuasive skills?

This question is a positive alternative to the query, "You don't seem to have all the experience I want; why should I hire you?" Even when you are presented with the question in this way, reply alertly. Break the question into two parts so that you are not tempted to make a long, boring statement. You also have the added benefit of drawing the interviewer into concurrence with your reply.

Start by saying, *"In my opinion, this position requires the following talents and skills . . . correct?"* List the skills briefly and then stop. If you do this in a gentle way, you can get the interviewer's buy-in.

Proceed carefully in case the interviewer is distracted or feels that you are now quizzing him. The second reason to be extremely careful is so that, when you list the talents and skills (in addition to persuasive skills), you select and emphasize those that play to your strengths. Avoid making a list that suggests that the job may overwhelm you.

I feel that my current position demands many skills, and I have been able to meet the demands thus far with great success. My special ability to be a quick learner and to be intuitive about other people's ability has enabled me to react to situations as needed.

If the interviewer cites a skill that you apparently do not have and that she feels is essential to the position, unless it is an obvious one, ask what aspect of the job requires it. You may cause the interviewer to rethink the job, reconsider the job requirements, or open the door to alternative skills or experience that you do have.

It is true that I do not have hands-on experience with InDesign, but I learned Dreamweaver quickly, so I feel confident that it will not take me an extensive amount of time to become proficient.

7.42 What would you do if you had to make a decision without a procedure or precedent to guide you?

This is a question to determine whether you have the ability to think for yourself and on your own two feet. The question is posed to determine your level of flexibility. Do you need rules all the time, or will you be lost? Are you the kind of person who will blend into our environment?

When reviewing your experience, you will have prepared for this question by considering what environment you prefer to work in: one with few rules and the excitement of the unknown, or a more staid environment in which rules and procedures provide a very structured environment for conducting business.

SHOW THAT YOU ARE A "CAN DO" CANDIDATE

❑ **There is no substitute for experience.** Study your work history to evaluate your types of experience.

❑ **Be honest.** If you do not have the kind of experience that is desired, do not invent it. Is there a comparable job skill or experience that you can offer?

❑ Should you find yourself lacking experience for which there is no substitute, **start getting training now.** Attend workshops, classes, Webinars, conferences, and seminars.

❑ **Become known in your field.** Join and take an active role in professional organizations. Attend conferences and become acquainted with as many of your peers as possible.

❑ **Share your knowledge** by teaching and doing workshops and seminars.

❑ **Get out every day,** even if it's only for a walk or a meal.

8

HOW WILL YOU FIT IN?

(OR WILL YOU?)

One increasingly popular way of determining a candidate's effectiveness is through the use of behavioral questions. Proponents of the behavioral approach contend that *past performance is the best predictor of future performance* ("can do" = "will do" again). In behavioral questioning, the interviewer asks applicants to supply experiences with situations that they will face if they are offered a position with the organization. This is back to our "can do," "will do," and "fit"—the underlying theme of all hiring.

Behaviors are actions (or reactions) in a situation, and the thinking is that similar behavior can be expected if a similar situation occurs. Hence, these questions ask, "Tell me about . . .," "Was there a time when . . . ?," or "Describe what you did when . . ." In addition to essentially making you take a test drive, these questions can give you insight into the organization or the position. A lot of questions regarding how you handle stress or difficult customers might hint at what the organization's priorities might be, for example.

When trying to determine the prospective effectiveness of an applicant, employers usually attempt to consider all the elements of the job. Skill assessment may be discussed in the interview process, but specific skills (which could be mentioned on a résumé or job application) should be tested more specifically, because talk is a poor substitute for action.

Language skills requirements are a major opportunity for interviewers to drop the ball when hiring a person because the language skills mentioned on the résumé are not put to the test until after the person starts the new job. Another danger area is equipment proficiency. Applicants can say that they can operate a piece of equipment, and references can be checked to verify that the applicant was employed in a position in which these skills were presumably utilized, but the employer never knows until after the candidate is hired if she can really do it—unless a work sample test is provided during the selection process. Another vulnerable area is software expertise. Frequently job boards include proficiency in one or more software programs in the job requirement section. However, most organizations do not test for the level of proficiency and are doomed to find out only after they hire the person.

One way to prepare for questions in this area is to consider all the "behaviors" that you (and you hope the organization) feel are essential to the job. *Behaviors are activities that are required for effective job performance.* Activities such as filing, sorting, and listing need to be given in more detail in order to provide specific examples from your past when you exhibited these behaviors. What was filed, how the material was received, and why it was stored would all be included. Additionally, the technology would be discussed, and details would be provided to describe whether the material was filed on hard drives, online, or in physical filing cabinets.

What distinguishes questions about behaviors from the "personal" questions discussed in Chapter 5? *Behavioral questions* are work-based and try to link the job applicant's past behaviors to behaviors that are required in the new job. They often pose a "What if . . ." or "Tell me about . . ." scenario, and they open the door for you to relate incidents that highlight the behavior they are inquiring about. They constitute a unique form of questioning based on the belief that past behaviors in similar or identical situations are clues to future performance in the environment for which the candidate is being considered. These questions can be more challenging for some applicants in that they require an assessment of prior experiences, distilling the essential behaviors utilized, being able to relate them to the current job opening, and telling all this in a concise, interesting manner. That's no mean feat.

If you have details about the position or if you can hypothesize what the behaviors needed in the position might be, you can prepare a "Behavior Worksheet" (see page 128). List any and all essential behaviors required for the position for which you are applying in as much detail as you can. Next, consider the relative importance of each of these behaviors to the organization and rank them. In the column next to each behavior, cite a job or a situation from your experience that also required you to be able to perform that behavior. This chart will identify your weak spots and allow you to consider in advance how your strengths and weaknesses may affect your "fit" for the position. Do not limit yourself to task-related behaviors, such as answering telephones, using a fax machine, or being able to word process (not "type") 60 wpm; include other important behaviors, such as delegating, scheduling, and organizing. When considering the behaviors required in the open position, look for alternatives in your own background. For some ideas, see the following list:

Administer	Assign	Advise	Brainstorm
Budget	Calculate	Coach	Coordinate
Create	Delegate	Design	Draft
Evaluate	Identify	Initiate	Lead
Lecture	Negotiate	Problem-solve	Reason
Reevaluate	Summarize	Theorize	Test
Update	Vindicate	Write	

BEHAVIOR WORKSHEET

Organization: _____ Date: _____
Position Applied For: _____
Rank behaviors from most essential (#1) to least essential (#5)

Essential Behaviors Required	Ranking	Details: Date and Job

---

*8.1   What is your management style? Provide examples from your current (or most recent) position that demonstrate this style.

You should have already considered this question as part of your self-assessment in preparation for any job search effort. *There are two major approaches; one emphasizes tasks, and the other stresses relationships.* They are not necessarily mutually exclusive, nor should they ever be, according to the management ex-

---

perts. In a traditional sense, managers are portrayed as being in a maintenance mode and reactive in a bureaucratic setting; leaders, on the other hand, are considered proactive individuals who look for problems and issues before they occur, and are results-driven and entrepreneurial in their thinking. In actuality, effective managers need to be talented leaders, since their objective is always to get things done through others, but this is a topic for another book.

The four major characteristics of management—planning, organizing, leading, and controlling—seem to have survived the test of time; various management theories may be considered within this context and still be complete. TQM (total quality management), reengineering, and benchmarking are all tools for managers to use when executing each of their major functions; they can be found in the titles of many recent bestsellers on management.

Leadership, on the other hand, has become a popular term to suggest the new approach that effective managers must now embrace if they are to be effective in this new, highly competitive environment with a diverse workforce taking a global approach to the marketplace. Interviewers may use the terms *manager* and *leader* interchangeably. So clarify which you are talking about if you feel that you and the interviewer are not both discussing the same attributes.

With that as background, think about your management style before the interview. Use the "Are You a Manager or a Leader?" questionnaire (see page 130) to help you consider the differences in approach. The higher the position you are interviewing for, the more insightful your leadership qualities are expected to be. Even if this is an entry-level position, be ready with an answer.

To prepare for this question, first consider the traits of the people you most frequently remember as great managers and determine what made them great. Think also about terrible managers for whom you have worked and what made them terrible. Then move on to yourself. Regardless of your professional level, consider a situation in which you had the opportunity to get things done through others (that's what management is all about) and recall what made you effective or ineffective. Did you communicate effectively? Did you stress teamwork? Did you emphasize quality and/or results? Did you get your hands dirty? Now try an answer that says yes to all of these:

I am a hands-on manager who stresses the importance of ongoing communication in building a team that delivers high-quality results.

Leadership is really the third characteristic of the management function, the one responsible for directing (or leading) the activities of others. It is of particular importance when we are talking about a participatory style of management because, rather than just expecting the workers to "do," it involves them in the organizing, planning, and controlling aspects of the function. What, then, is left for the manager to do? Direct or lead.

Use the word *we* rather than *I* to demonstrate that you give credit for accomplishments to the team that you say is so important to your managerial effectiveness (if that is what you mentioned). A survey reported in the media states that 57 percent of executives feel that having poor team-playing skills is the easiest way to kill a career.

ARE YOU A MANAGER OR A LEADER?

Compare column A to column B. For each row, mark a Yes for the statement that your work style agrees with.

A	B
___ Do you work within boundaries?	___ Do you expand boundaries?
___ Do you control resources?	___ Do you influence others?
___ Are you making plans to reach goals?	___ Are you working to create a future?
___ Are you responsible for when and how work is done?	___ Do you commit to getting the work done at any cost?
___ Are you ruled by reason and logic supported by intuition?	___ Are you ruled by intuition and feelings supported by reason?
___ Do the past and precedents dictate your present actions?	___ Does your vision for the future dictate your present actions?
___ Do you make decisions only after all relevant information is available?	___ Do you decide when you feel you have enough (even if not all) information?
___ Do you measure performance against plans?	___ Do you measure accomplishments against your vision of the future?

Scoring: Yes answers in column A indicate management qualities, while those in column B pertain to leadership.

LEADERSHIP/MANAGEMENT SKILL ASSESSMENT

Provide five examples of leadership or management and state when and where you exhibited them:

	WHEN	WHERE
1.		
2.		
3.		
4.		
5.		

MARKS OF A GREAT TEAM PLAYER

- ❏ **Plays** fair.
- ❏ **Accepts** responsibility for problems while giving credit to others for successes.
- ❏ **Shares** compliments with team members.
- ❏ **Supports** decisions (even when not happy about them).
- ❏ **Offers** constructive criticism.
- ❏ **Is optimistic** in tough situations.

8.2   Are you a good manager? Give some examples to demonstrate that.

Consider each of the four major characteristics cited earlier—planning, organizing, leading, and controlling—and determine which one best provides examples that demonstrate your management ability. Now is the time to tell a story that shows you "in action."

Relocation expenses were out of control when I took responsibility for the function. I reviewed the reports [controlling], and worked with seasoned staff members to determine the key entry points to maximize efforts and contain expenses. They made a series of recommendations [directing], and we drafted a plan. We then set up a work flow system to maximize the effectiveness of the new procedures [organizing].

If you say "no" in response to the interviewer's question, "Are you a good manager?" you won't get the job—unless it just so happens, as it does occasionally, that an astute interviewer is asking the question because the last thing the organization wants is a good manager; it needs a hands-on doer instead. In these times of major downsizing, most organizations, even for their manager positions, want hands-on persons who will do a lot of the job themselves. Even in this situation, it is safer to say:

I am good at both—being a good manager and being a "solo practitioner." I have been in both situations throughout my career, and I have learned to be effective at both.

Do not panic if you have never managed in a paid capacity; chances are that you have done so either personally with your family or as part of voluntary or community activities. Prepare, before the meeting, to identify situations that you were personally involved in that demanded management expertise. If you are a recent college graduate, consider any organizations that you held a title in or any activities (a dance, raffle, or concert) that you actively worked to promote. Determine which of the duties that you performed required help from others.

*8.3 How do/did you interact differently with diverse management levels and types?

You need to show that you are accustomed to interacting with people at different management levels. Refresh your memory by reviewing your "Job History Worksheet" (see page 41) with its "Organization" section.

Indicate with a brief answer the variety of unit heads that you have had to deal with, and on what issues. If you are seeking employment with a global organization, now is the time to share any expertise or experience dealing with international companies, cultures, or personnel.

8.4 How far do you see yourself rising in our organization?

Be realistic. If you can be vague and you want to take that tack, certainly do so: *"I would like to rise as high as my skills and opportunities here permit."* If that works and there is no follow-up question, you are off the hook. However, chances are that you need to provide a little more detail.

Consider your field of expertise as one avenue: *"I would like to eventually be responsible for the marketing function, or become CFO, or any other title for a major function, or even chairman of the board."* Note that the answer states a title with a function attached; to answer *"I am hoping to be at the vice presidential level in five years"* omits what you will have an expertise in at that level. Make sure that the goal is appropriate and that you feel confident sharing this information with the interviewer. It is also an opportunity to show what you have learned about the organization, either through research or by listening during the interview.

*8.5 What is your relationship with your former employer?

"We continue to keep in touch" is a nice way to start if that is the truth. If it isn't, do not worry, because a continuing relationship with a former employer is, under usual circumstances, as difficult to maintain as a relationship with a divorced spouse. *"We haven't spoken* [or, better, *we have occasionally spoken] since I left, but they know they are free to call if a situation requires my attention."* Sometimes an employer of a departing employee invites the ex-employee back for consulting assignments. If this is true, say so, because this scenario suggests a real respect for the applicant, and that message will be heard.

*8.6 Describe a situation in which the team fell apart. What was your role in the outcome?

Do not be concerned here about the "failure" aspect of the question. The interviewer wants an idea, based on your experience, of how you deal with adversity: *first, that you recognize problems when they occur, and second, that you are able do something about them.*

> *As the manager of a training facility for _____, I was unable to solve serious attendance problems with more than 20 instructors who were primarily single parents. The problem was not just one of replacement requirements when an instructor was late or took an unscheduled day off, but the amount of bickering among the workers increased as the problem intensified. I identified a two-pronged solution. First, I made one person responsible for time and attendance records; second, I gave the instructors an incentive that many would regard as puny: any staff member with no lateness and no unexcused absence for a period of six months would be entitled to a half day off. It worked because the staff members really valued any time that they had to themselves.*

*8.7   Describe a situation in which the person you were dealing with enabled you to be more effective.

Think win-win. Consider this example:

> *I joined a smaller, privately held entertainment company after spending several years at a major, publicly traded music company with foreign ownership. Now, when I dealt with my direct report, the company's president, she was pleased at the swiftness of issue resolutions for major decisions involving the department's budget and marketing campaigns. Going from a pressure-cooker environment to one where skills were appreciated and relationships could be developed was such a pleasure. This was due to the president's quick, positive response to my efforts.*

*8.8   Describe a situation in which you needed to get an understanding of another person's viewpoint before you could get your job done. What problems did you encounter, and how did you handle them?

Consider a situation in which you and a colleague had a major difference of opinion regarding an action plan or a definition of a problem that you were both expected to solve. This kind of scenario can frequently be used to address this question. What frequently exacerbates the problem is a personality conflict, and the working relationship may be marred by non-work-related issues. Whatever you do, *never identify a scenario that may lead the interviewer to think that you may be the problem,* because the questions raised about where the real problem may lie will be greater and more memorable than the issues that the story is intended to resolve.

> *A build-out on a new lease was loaded with problems that included delays. The designer did not get along with the construction manager, who did not get along with the property management team. Our facilities manager, who reported to me, was an effective employee, but these complicated relationship challenges were beyond his expertise. After clarifying the agendas of the four major leaders of this project, I worked with the facilities manager to be sure that he understood the perspective of each of the other three leaders. In addition, he had to see that the project would be completed successfully only if he, as the person who had ownership of the project, could get the others to see that only by their working together would the project be completed on time and at (or under) budget. As his manager, I coached him through this thought process. Only when I saw that he bought in did I encourage him to reach out to the others to concentrate on the project and*

bury their differences. I then stepped back but continued to follow the progress of the project through periodic meetings with the facilities manager.

8.9 How did you feel the last time you joined a new organization and met your new group?

A balanced comment is a demonstration of a realistic approach on your part. You need to feel optimistic, but at the same time it is not surprising if you detect a "show us" attitude.

Although I have changed jobs only three times, I feel excited at the prospect of starting a new position. A key component of that excitement is meeting the new team members. However, the last time, my new boss had warned me that the group was skeptical of all newcomers. Before being introduced, I asked my boss to share with them that my experience at _____ would help me to add value right from the start. The name of the organization and the comment from her went a long way toward helping to set the tone for first impressions. For a few days after that, each of the team members approached me and asked me to share my experiences at _____.

8.10 It seems as if it has been a long time since you changed jobs. How do you feel about joining a new group/new organization?

With questions like this, it is all about a positive response.

As we already discussed, this recent job search was brought about by circumstances outside my control, and I have decided to see it as an opportunity. Your _____ appears innovative and energetic, exactly the kind of group that I feel I can quickly contribute to. An opportunity to work here cannot be anything other than exciting.

8.11 If we were to hire you, what do you think would be the first things on your "to do" list on day 1?

Because of the great similarity between the position here and my current position, I would want to see exactly how the work flowed from the designers to the editors and then onto the Web site. I know that having a working system for the data is crucial to the content and images on the Web site, and I would also seek to meet all the people performing the specific functions in the department to see how they work together.

*8.12 Tell me about a difficult situation when you pulled the team together.
Identify a situation that led to a positive outcome, and be careful during the answering of the question to mix your *we* and *I* pronouns to demonstrate that you were an active participant in the group. When you can, quantify your responses: the size of the team, the budgetary amounts involved, the time frame of the project—all of these will help the interviewer "see" you in action.

> *When one of the members of our five-person team, and the most highly regarded, resigned, I had to break the news not only that she was leaving, but that she would not be replaced. I then told the team that we would meet in two days to map out a strategy to determine how we were going to accomplish the same results with only four people. Then for the next two days (right up to the meeting), I visited each person (including the departing employee) to assess that person's morale and level of concern—as well as his or her willingness to identify and participate in a new work process. Individually I mentioned to each of them that the business was going through a downturn, and that we really needed each person's input and participation if we were to continue as a work group and help the organization to get through this difficult time in its life cycle. I must have gotten through because two of the members brought doughnuts and one of them stated at the beginning of the meeting that they had been discussing this situation among themselves, and they wanted me to know that they realized the tough situation that I was in and that they were giving me their total support and attention because we were going to get through this together.*

8.13   When you begin to work with new people, how do you get to understand them? Are you successful in predicting/interpreting their behavior? Give examples.
Listening is the key to getting to understand another person. When you start with a new work group, its members have an advantage over you: they need to understand just one new person—you. You, on the other hand, must get to understand each and every one of them. In addition, even with excellent listening skills, it is still difficult to predict a person's behavior each and every time. To answer this question in a strong, confident manner, it is important for you to say at the start that you have had a great deal of success in predicting and interpreting other people's behavior, but also mention that it does not always work. Then proceed with a brief example or two.

*An MBA we had hired needed to be told that one of her responsibili-
ties would include spending some time each day on the switchboard.
She said that she felt we were going to have this discussion, and she
realized that because we were short-staffed, she would be expected to
put in time on telephone coverage. This was not a surprise because
during the recruiting and selection process, we had emphasized in our
discussions the "hands-on" and "do whatever we have to" atmosphere
that is a key to the culture of our organization, and she had confirmed
throughout that she realized that this was something that she might be
called upon to do once she joined us.*

*8.14 Tell me about a responsibility in your current/last job that you really enjoyed.

Be careful not to throw this gift question away. Even though it should be easy,
carefully determine your answer in advance. This is sometimes a "one-two" question that is immediately followed by a request for you to identify the responsibility that you really liked least.

Ideally, you should concentrate on the most important aspects of your position—the most creative, the most project-oriented, the most essential to the organization—or a responsibility that is very similar to one that you would assume
in the new position. A very senior member of the management of one of the
world's major banks used to always say, "An organization can never have enough
good people. If you meet one as a job applicant and you don't have a job to offer,
hire him or her, make the hire anyway, and find something for the person to do."
Too frequently, however, interviewers are more interested in *screening out* rather
than *screening in*, and *this question could be the decision maker*. If you are being
considered for a position that is well below your last one, you may be giving the
interviewer an opportunity to dismiss you.

*In my ___ years with _____, I had several jobs, and I was fortu-
nate to have many opportunities to learn and grow on the job. The
one responsibility that I enjoyed the most was one that was not overtly
stated: the responsibility to train others that I worked with and develop
their opportunities.*

*8.15 Give an example of a situation where you had to be assertive/cre-ative/supportive on the job.

This question gives interviewers the opportunity to determine how you exhibit
a certain characteristic that they feel is essential to the position. You should be
well prepared for this question, having reviewed your "Behavior Worksheet" (see

page 127). Given the list that you prepared, what additional characteristics do you feel are essential to the job or detrimental to your candidacy?

Depending on the trait and the interviewer's agenda, *this question can either screen candidates in or screen them out*. A given trait can be viewed either as a *positive* or as a *negative*. Take, for example, the adjectives *creative* and *aggressive*. Creativity in an advertising manager is a laudable trait; in an accountant, creative bookkeeping entries could cause problems. Aggressiveness in a sales manager who pushes into new markets could be exactly what a start-up company needs, but aggressiveness is not what a child-care agency requires. All positions should be viewed as offering opportunities to exhibit most personal traits, and a particular trait can be a greater or lesser part of the position's responsibility. For the creative accountant, a response could be:

> *I find that all the different types of clients and their individual business needs require a creative mind to solve their problems. No two clients are alike, and I feel that the secret to my success is making them feel that they are getting individual service created for their individual needs.*

8.16 Describe a complex problem that you had to deal with.

To prepare an answer to this question, refer to your "Experience Worksheet" (see pages 101–102) and your "Critical Incidents Worksheet" (see page 103). When reviewing your accomplishments, select one of the most meaningful and consider it in terms of its level of complexity. Pick a situation that shows you to be an effective organizational player. For the word *problem*, substitute *project* if it helps to clarify appropriate situations.

> *A senior person was hired as revenue director for a health-care organization. This important position required an effective work flow process that would, as a final step, lead to timely payments accurately covering all services provided. The challenge for this newcomer was that she was only one element in the operation, and for her to do her job, each of the subunits had to perform effectively. After a very short time, she realized that referrals were falling, and that this would, of course, affect payments on the back end. She approached me, as her coach, to help her deal effectively with this matter. When I suggested that she consider utilizing a member of the faculty of a nearby college as a consultant to do a work flow analysis, she saw right away that this would minimize finger-pointing and allow her to provide an objective overview to her boss, and that it would be an opportunity to identify (from an outsider's view) the bottlenecks in the operation cycle.*

8.17   Describe a situation in which you failed to reach a goal.

Interviewers try to determine how you deal with adversity and to see whether you have a need to win every time. If possible, identify a situation in which you had to adjust your sights, then went back to succeed at a later date. Succeeding, however, is not as important as your demonstration of the ability to deal with tough times as well as good.

College may be one example, for instance, if you had to delay higher education because of personal circumstances. Do not let bitterness come through.

I had hoped to work at night while attending classes during the day to complete my college education, but the high cost of living caused me to have to work full-time just to support myself. I was fortunate to have an employer that switched my schedule to daytime, and I attended classes in the evenings and weekends. It took me longer to get my degree, but I always felt that I valued my education more because I had really had to "earn" to learn. My business courses also related to my day-to-day activities on the job.

I had submitted a training program proposal to a local bank at its request. Many meetings were held, with senior management requesting revisions in the program, which I accommodated. The meetings never resulted in a signed contract, however, because the HR manager quit in the midst of the negotiations to work at another bank. The timing was not good to push the proposal forward at that time. A few years passed, and the replacement's replacement, in cleaning out drawers, found my proposal. She contacted me; we had one meeting and then signed a contract. One point she made in discussing the original proposal with me was how willing I had been to meet the specific needs of the bank.

8.18   Describe circumstances in which you had to work under pressure and deal with deadlines.

This should be an easy one for everyone, but do not take it for granted. Review your worksheets and consider the best, most recent story that the interviewer is most likely to relate to. If this is the essence of your daily activities, mention that fact and discuss the various deadlines and pressures that you need to deal with on a regular and daily basis. This is just as true, if not even more so, for those who are returning to the workplace. With many projects to deal with and soft lines of responsibility, the pressure may be greater, and the deadlines may sometimes be ignored until a crisis develops.

If you cannot think of such a situation either at work or in your personal life, seek assistance from a relative, friend, or colleague. The experiences are there; it just takes sensitivity to identify them.

It looked as if my suggestion that we commence a performance review exercise for each of the employees of the organization for the calendar year just ending was not going to take place. All of a sudden, however, the CEO asked for a performance management program and gave me two hours to prepare it. It would not have been helpful to ask for more time, and at the same time I knew that the CEO was not asking for a finished plan, but merely for a first draft. In two hours she had a performance appraisal form, which then became the frame of reference for the discussion on performance management that went forward with the rest of the executive management team. That discussion led to a brainstorming session on goals and salary increases. The result was that in three weeks, we had put together a program, with a training component that was instrumental in meeting sales goals in a very weak economy, and it all started with a two-hour deadline.

8.19 You must have had problems with _____. How did you handle these problems?

You are being asked to demonstrate your specific work experience and mirror the situation the interviewer is describing. You need to focus on his description of the situation. Your answer has to not only demonstrate your comprehension of the question, but briefly and succinctly provide a cogent answer as well. If you have a "been there, done that" experience, now is the time to highlight it. If the interviewer has indeed hit on a common problem, it also shows that he has been listening and has some insight into the position.

When we downsized, I did have problems with coverage. And I knew that the remaining staff members would be concerned that in addition to the extra work, they would also have to cover the reception area. Since we are a nonprofit, we have the opportunity to use volunteers, so I contacted the Volunteers' Office to see if we would be eligible for a volunteer to help with coverage. The staff appreciated my efforts, although it took a while before we finally received our volunteer. He did so well, and he got along with the staff so much, that they encouraged him to apply for a job, which he did and was ultimately hired.

8.20 Describe a situation in which you had a personal commitment that conflicted with an emergency business meeting. What did you do?

This question seeks to determine your level of loyalty and your involvement in family issues or other outside interests. You need to answer directly and unhesitatingly.

I would have to make arrangements to be sure that the personal commitment is taken care of by someone else.

You may even add,

I always try to warn anyone that I deal with outside the organization that any commitment is subject to change if my employer requires it.

If you have an example of a situation that shows what lengths you will go to in your commitment to the organization, give it. Here is one example:

I was a frequent workshop speaker for a major professional organization. The organization realized that I should have a backup, and it had found a few who could fill in in an emergency. While I was at a workshop, I was required to return. Even though the professional organization had backups, none of them was available. To resolve the matter, I arranged a teleconference session in order to ensure that the professional organization met its commitment, but also, and more important, so that I was present for a meeting back at headquarters.

8.21 How do you establish priorities?

There is no one "right answer" for this. Different jobs require different methods; how a surgeon establishes priorities is different from how a chef does, for example. Consider your experience and what you imagine to be the routine of the new job, and give a response that shows your flexibility.

I start and end each day by reviewing my "to do" list. Some tasks are time-sensitive or can be best completed at certain times, like telephone calls to Europe in the morning and to our West Coast offices in the late afternoon. Clients are always a priority; problems come up and need to be handled immediately, so a lot of flexibility is needed. Staying late when days go off-track is a fact of life.

BE ON YOUR BEST "BEHAVIOR"

❑ **Be objective;** know yourself.

❑ **Answer the questions directly;** do not ramble.

❑ **Provide details and quantify your answers** so that the interviewer can get a complete picture.

❑ Use the **appropriate vocabulary** level; do not overuse jargon. Do not use dated references or terminology.

❑ **Speak** about **concepts and people** as much as about facts and things.

❑ **Listen** as much as you talk.

❑ **Stress facts** rather than conjecture.

❑ Use **we** instead of **I** to stress a team approach.

9

HOW MANY WAYS CAN YOU SPELL *STRESS?*

The Central Intelligence Agency and law enforcement agencies sometimes submit candidates to one or more stress tests to determine whether the candidate is "tough enough" to handle a grueling job. Some TV shows, such as *Hell's Kitchen*, seem to think that stress is part of the kitchen experience. Other organizations and individuals (not associated with spying or law enforcement) also sometimes come to the conclusion that "stress interviews" are an effective technique for evaluating job candidates, even though research results repeatedly demonstrate that stress interviews are *not* valid predictors of job performance. Many people who are looking for a job contend that all recruitment and selection interviews are stressful enough without having specific questions that are aimed at raising the discomfort level.

For any individual, there are subjects that may be raised in the course of an interview that personally cause stress. They may make you feel uncomfortable, and you may have only a modicum of control over disclosure. Talking about losing your job, coming out of a terrible work situation, being in the midst of a long, unfruitful job search, or the ever-delicate subject of compensation can make many a job candidate sweat. There are questions that are chosen to put candidates in the "hot seat," but there are others that "push our buttons." The trick is to not engage those panic buttons while you are in the interview by anticipating that these questions may pop up.

Stress—the Ever-Present Factor in the Employment Process

Whether the employer consciously decides to inject it or not, stress can permeate the employment process in every organization as it attempts to find the right candidate for each position that it seeks to fill.

The interview itself can be a stressful experience for any job candidate (and also, possibly, for the interviewer). In addition, the surroundings may contribute.

Asking a job candidate to fill out an application without a clipboard or, worse, a pen may be an agonizing experience for the person who has no flat surface available on which to complete the application.

Even the furniture may contribute to stress. A U.S. subsidiary of a major Japanese bank had futons available for job applicants in its human resources reception area. There were no other choices. It was futons or stand. The futons were easy enough to sit on, and comfortable, too. The problem, though, was that they were impossible to get up from without some very awkward moments for both male and female candidates.

The receptionist and other staff members who come into contact with job candidates may provide additional opportunities for stress. There is the story of the HR vice president who, when passing through the reception area for the third time in three hours, noticed the same person still sitting in the same place. When she asked the receptionist why the applicant was still sitting there, he responded, "How should I know? If he doesn't know enough to come to me and give me his completed application, that's his problem." Even though the receptionist was let go the next day, it was one day too late for the erstwhile applicant.

Stress Makers	Stress Breakers
The interview itself	Prepare; know your material
Silence during the interview; internal pressure to keep talking	Accept silence; avoid being intimidated to speak more; control disclosure
An offer to smoke or have a beverage	Limit your chances for further anxiety by saying, "No thanks"
Mealtime interview	Recognize that you are not there to eat, you are there to get a job; order simply
An inexperienced, antagonistic, rushed, late, unprepared, or bored interviewer	Be adaptable; offer clear, concise answers; read body language to see if you are getting your points across

What are your personal stress makers? What are your plans to reduce the stress that these cause in advance?

My Stressors	My Solutions

*9.1 What can I do for you? Why did you ask to meet with me?

The fact that such a question may come up is one more reason for being sure of your objective for any meeting and for sharing that objective with the person you want to meet with. Before going to any meeting, have a clear idea of the interviewer's role in the selection process and the objective of the meeting. *When this "intimidating" question is asked, there should be no doubt as to the purpose of the meeting.* In appropriate situations, mention directly that you are hoping the person that you are meeting with will offer you a job, or at least consider you a "pass-along."

You should do everything you can to avoid the term *informational interview*, and also make a habit of avoiding these interviews. The informational interview is an opportunity for job applicants to gather data; they have chosen to "pick the person's brain." What nerve to assume that the person you have contacted buys in to your request to give you time for your purposes. It is further complicated by the fact that many job search books encourage you to request this as an excuse to get an interview, then, once you are there, to try to get a job—so your real intent is not to pick the person's brain, but to get a job without saying so! In our minds, that is really a deceptive practice—not a way that we would suggest you start a relationship.

This becomes even more of a problem when interviewers ask what they can do for you. Does it make sense to say that you are only looking for data? If the interviewer has a job available, he may not share that fact with you when you claim to be interested only in gathering information. If you really want a job and say so, then you have lowered your camouflage, and you may make the interviewer wonder if he agreed to the interview under false pretenses.

Note: Informational interviews are frequently encouraged by outplacement specialists and other career counselors, but they are problematic because they have a confused agenda. Their justification is to stimulate interest in the job seeker and develop a network of contacts by making a direct statement up front that the purpose of this meeting is not to generate a job offer. If anything, the interview should be called a *courtesy* interview instead. What confuses the meeting is the question of who is the interviewer. Job seekers in this instance are really the interviewers because they are interested in obtaining information, but job holders become the interviewers if they are expected to refer the applicant to others and elsewhere. If it is a courtesy interview, the objective is to extend the courtesy of a meeting, and the conversation determines the interviewer's next step, if any (a referral, a direction, or a publication).

If you have spoken honestly to the person you are meeting with about the true purpose of the meeting, you might say, for example, *"I was hoping that I would be able to convince you that I am a person that your organization would love to hire."*

An alternative is to *ask for the names of others that you will be able to reach out to in your job search.* Again, this seems to us like an unfair imposition and one that requires more time from the person who has just taken the time to meet with you.

*9.2 Are you free to travel? Willing to relocate? Able to work weekends or evenings?

Don't be intimidated. Agree if you are willing to do so. Take the question or topic as an opportunity for negotiation. Don't immediately say "yes" without qualification, but seek details and more information first. It is reasonable to ask:

What is overtime like here? How frequent is it?

Will I get paid for overtime worked? If so, on what basis [comp time or cash; straight time and/or time and a half or more]?

For travel, find out the types of location, frequency, and reimbursement methods. Consider the details of any commitments regarding entertainment at home before saying yes. You are perceived as a more knowledgeable person if you do so.

Caution: There may also be a hidden illegal agenda. The interviewer may suspect that you are of a religious persuasion that prohibits you from working overtime at certain times during the week. This matter is discussed from that perspective in Chapter 11, "Don't Go There!"

*9.3   Do you have any questions? What else can I tell you?

A really weak answer is, *"No, you have already answered all of them during the interview."* To the interviewer, this may sound like, *"I do not want to be bothered making the effort to ask any questions"* or *"I just want to get out of here."* Keep in mind that the interviewer is probably interested in learning more about you by using your questions to gain more of an appreciation of who you are. Don't rush the relationship by asking about benefits, vacation entitlements, or bonuses; those are part of negotiations *after* the job has been offered.

Before every interview, as part of your preparation, you should make a list of questions or gaps in the information you have regarding the organization or position (for further discussion, see Chapter 12, "Now It Is Your Turn: Questions to Raise"). This preparation accomplishes four objectives:

1. By making this process a habit, job applicants quickly become adept at identifying the information they need from every interview.
2. When they have prepared their questions in advance, no matter when this question is popped, applicants are ready to go.
3. By preparing their questions in advance, applicants increase the likelihood that their questions will be answered, but with prepared questions they can truly concentrate on the answers.
4. In reviewing the responses and how forthcoming the interviewer was in answering your questions, you will be able to further evaluate the organization and position if a job offer is made.

If you do not have a question ready when you are asked for one, here are two that you might consider to get the interviewer talking.

- *"How's business?"*
- *"Please share with me what you like best about working here."*

Note that both of these questions are open-ended requests for information that provide two very important items of information for you as part of your due diligence process. The first is a good question for you to ask if you want to know in what phase of its life cycle the organization is currently situated. You may want to rethink your interest in working at a place if it is currently undergoing a major decline and is in its last stage of its organizational life. The second usually stimulates a good response, since you are getting the interviewer to discuss something that is usually number one on the list of things she likes to discuss—herself.

9.4 Don't you think you would be better suited to a different size/type of company?

What does this question mean? Most probably, the interviewer either has written you off or is baiting you. In either instance, *avoid going on the defensive by taking the offensive: "What makes you say that?"* Be careful, and try to determine what made the interviewer raise the question in the first place. You might even respond with the comment, *"Please share with me your reason for your opinion."* Listen carefully for the answer, and avoid reacting (be careful to keep your emotions in check), but identify, as we mention later, the appropriate response.

In your preparation, completing the "Job History Worksheet" (see page 41), "My Ideal Job" (see page 42), the "Organization Fact Sheet" (see page 50), and the "Behavior Worksheet" (see page 127) should have convinced you that you are interviewing for the right job at the right organization. Now you need to convince the interviewer of the "fit" of your candidacy. If the interviewer is concentrating on the differences between your past experience and the hiring organization, seek to point out areas of similarity. This should also be part of your preparation—looking for common areas of your past and the position the organization has available.

> *It is true that I have worked primarily for large, global organizations, but in my current position, our division was run much like a smaller company, much like yours. We had budgets that I worked on both for controlling expenses and for increasing our market penetration. We worked with local ad agencies to develop pertinent campaigns to attract customers, and we dealt with local vendors whenever possible.*

9.5 How do you think this interview is going?

Try to stay realistic in your comments. You have nothing to lose because the interviewer is asking your opinion. So you cannot be incorrect. *"I feel uncomfortable in that you do not seem interested in my experience. Am I answering your questions in sufficient detail?"* The worst statement could be the comment that you feel the interview is going well when it is not. Again, be sure to seek affirmation from the interviewer. By asking for the interviewer's thoughts at the end of your answer, you will get some feedback. Take it.

9.6 This appears to be a career change for you. Why do you think it is a good choice?

If this is a good move for you, then your reasons should also seem good to an interviewer; if you are grasping at straws and are honestly looking for any job that you can get, this will come out sooner or later, so it's best to justify your approach prior to the interview.

The best way to prepare for this eventual topic of discussion is to make your own list of reasons why this is a good move: transferable skills, traits that both areas have in common, similarities in organizations/operations.

After buying paper from mills all across the United States and Europe for the past decade, I thought my experience and knowledge would be an easy transfer to selling paper here. I have a wealth of knowledge of the industry, and flipping to the other side of the transaction would give me a fresh outlook while using my experience to best advantage.

*9.7 How long have you been looking for a job?

The interviewer also may be thinking: "Why are you still looking for a job? Why haven't you found a job yet? Why does no one else want to hire you? Then, why should we consider hiring you?"

This stress-building question can easily intimidate you if you have not prepared for it. Take it for what it is, and give it a brief answer. Be consistent with any other information that you furnished on your application or résumé.

If it has obviously been some length of time since your last job, and this has been an undesirable fact of life for you, try to put a positive spin on it, even in the direst of circumstances. Most employers do not want to be faced with a desperate applicant. So try your best to avoid looking like one. Possible reasons to give for your continued unemployed status/extended job search are

- *"I am searching for the right opportunity."* You have not been looking for just another job where you might have to go through this process again after a short period of time.
- *"I am trying to find a real career opportunity with the right organization."* You have had offers, but for one reason or another, you preferred to continue your search. If you take this tack, be ready to support it with concrete examples of job offers that you passed up. Do not make the list too long, even if true; two or three examples should always suffice.
- *"I had personal matters to deal with."* As more and more people are living longer, the working population is more frequently placed in a position of providing assistance to those older than themselves as well as caring for

children. This is true not only for your immediate family, but for other relatives, neighbors, and friends (including friends of your parents) as well. State that you had personal matters to attend to and, rather than give less than your full attention to your job search, you felt that it was more appropriate for you to solve the immediate problem and then give all your energies to the search, which you are now doing.

- *"I am completing school."* Have you delayed the completion of your schooling in the past for whatever reason (finances, family, or other commitments, such as an obligation to take responsibility for managing the family's business)? Currently, more and more people are accepting the fact that the farther in the past you left school (whether you completed it or not), the less likely it is that the skills you learned are relevant. Cutting-edge thinking now is that education should be a never-ending process. By continuing school as an adult learner throughout your professional life, you are more likely to be current with the latest thinking in your subject areas. Whether the courses are job-related (especially directly) or not, you are perceived as a person who is interested in personal growth as an ongoing commitment and one who becomes excited by the thrill of the new.

- *"Consulting assignments have been keeping me busy."* This response may be considered an overused avenue to present. It is as if there is a universal rule of nature. Recruiters are always talking about all the out-of-work people they see who claim that they have been consulting while they were searching for a job. Just as we mentioned with educational pursuits, if this is the route you pursue, make sure that you have a complete story, because all but the most ill prepared, poorly trained, and least experienced (I think you get the point) interviewers will try to determine the veracity of your portrayal. Be ready not only to have a story, but to make it a good one (hopefully truthful), with a client profile, perhaps disclosing the industry, size, employee numbers, revenues, and/or number of work locations. You don't have to disclose the client's name. By creating a little mystery, you are stealing the interviewer's opportunity to evaluate the prestige of your client and to peg you in terms of professional stature. Also, if the interviewer is interested, be ready with a brief summary (very focused and very brief) of the nature of the engagement, including a comment about the result.

- Before we leave this response, let us suggest that if you are able and interested, you should give consulting a try while you are looking for a job. The assignment may lead to a job, for one thing. It is a résumé filler, for another. Third, it gives you an entrepreneurial edge. Fourth, consulting is a confidence builder, since folks who work in organizations that hire consultants tend to regard consultants as advanced experts in their fields. Finally not-for-profits and public-sector employers frequently seek out consultants to perform projects on a volunteer basis—something that does not require much marketing, since local contacts frequently are aware of such situations when, for whatever reason, the posts go unfilled.

- *"I am making a change in career."* If you mean it, then you have to do some research and lots of homework before you do so. Become focused and determine a plan of action for exploring your chosen path in more depth. You must anticipate booby traps. Is the job or organization that you are meeting with consistent with your new career? What activities have you pursued to quickly build up your knowledge in this new area? What about compensation? Do you expect at least to avoid a cut in pay, or is there an apprenticeship aspect that requires paying one's dues? Once you agree to that, though, will the prospective employer anticipate (or hope) that you can be obtained at a cheap price? If you are contemplating a career change, don't consider yourself odd or an exception. Charles Handy, in his popular book *The Age of Unreason*, says that at the present time, people on average go through at least three career changes (not jobs or organizations) in their lifetimes. So we should expect such cases. If you are thinking in these terms, pat yourself on the back because you are considering an action that makes you very contemporary.

- *"The job market/economy is very tight."* What is now called the Great Recession by some economists may depress the job market for a substantial time period, and interviewers may no longer look askance at applicants who have had extended job searches. Acknowledge the external environment and then move on to why the company should hire you.

Yes, it has been a tough time, but I know that I have a lot to offer, and the _____ position here at _____ is an ideal fit. My skills in _____ and experience with _____ will allow me to make a valuable contribution quickly. Meanwhile, I am using this time to also _____ (learn, study) _____.

9.8 How long will it take for you to make a meaningful contribution to our organization?

If you suggest too long a time frame, interviewers will wonder if you will ever make a contribution. Saying *"From day one!"* requires an explanation of what you can do for the organization immediately. Organizations recognize that any new employee is expected to have to go up the learning curve. The higher the level of the person hired, the more tolerant the organization is about expecting results, but in those instances, the later the impact, the greater the results. In no case should the time frame extend beyond six months.

> *I am sure that there are differences in production and operations that I need to pick up on, but my varied experiences with different business models will certainly allow a fast transition, and I feel that I will be pulling my full share in a week or so.*

If you readily see opportunities for improvement just from your observations during your visit, be certain that the person with whom you want to share these will be happy to hear of them. We suggest that you err here on the side of caution and refrain from sharing your comments on opportunities for improvement until you learn more about what the interviewer prefers doing and his reasons for doing so. Don't spend all your potential capital in the interview—leave yourself something to deliver after you are hired!

9.9   How long would you expect to stay with us?

You need to think about what is the right answer or the wrong answer for this "gotcha" question. Think about it. If you switched roles with your interviewer, what would you want to hear? Consider the organization you are meeting with and the timelines it considers appropriate. If you are meeting with a highly entrepreneurial company, you do not want to say something along the lines of, *"I am looking for a place to stay until I retire."* In most such cases, the sedentary and security-tinged tone of this answer will not be well received. Sometimes, however, circumstances can make this answer appropriate, even in an entrepreneurial environment. If, for instance, you are nearing retirement age, that would be a most effective answer regardless of the type of organization because it tells the employer that there is a specific limit to your stay. At the same time, you both know your intent up front.

Try to determine the "right" answer with your interviewer in mind, but be careful not to say something that would be inconsistent with the rest of your presentation. *"I have never been a job hopper. I plan to stay as long as there continue to be challenges."* With that answer, though, be ready for the follow-up: "What do we have to do to keep you challenged?" *"As long as I continue to learn"* is a troublesome reply because the tone suggests that the organization is responsible for your well-being, and you have now established a problem. The burden on the employer (if it hires you) is to constantly worry that you feel that you are always learning. Employers want applicants who bring solutions with them; they have enough problems already.

In a paternalistic organization, the culture is familylike. That is, you are carefully and constantly oriented to the organization, and the organization tries to do this effectively by blurring the lines between personal and professional. If this is a style that you prefer and you see it as the organization's approach, say, *"Considering that I have hoped to work here for ages, since my college years, I will be in no hurry to seek other alternatives."* Then explain that you see work as an opportunity to "belong" and that belonging to this great organization would be quite a coup.

For a more traditionally structured organization, a response such as this may be more appropriate:

> *We both seem to value innovation and creativity; I am so excited about the possibility of being involved with package design for the new product line you spoke of that I cannot imagine running out of ideas in the near future.*

*9.10 How many hours do/did you find it necessary to work each week to get your job done?

Portray yourself as someone who has a strong work ethic, but at the same time is not overwhelmed by work. *"It varies"* may be the perfect answer because it allows you next to mention that the usual amount of time that you put in each week is between 40 and 55 hours. You are then able to add a comment such as, *"The amount of actual time required depends on diverse factors; I have found being flexible and having a like-minded team to be the key to success."* If you feel comfortable ending the answer there, it is certainly acceptable and pleasingly brief.

*9.11 If our roles were reversed, what questions would you ask?

If you are ready for this question, usually only one question is required: ask the question that you feel is most relevant and that also affords you the opportunity to give a strong, positive, confident answer. Do not open the door to any topic that touches on your possible inappropriateness for the position and/or organization being discussed. The answer *"You have already covered all the questions very thoroughly"* or something to that effect is weak.

If you feel that you are well prepared, suggest either *"What can you do for us?"* or *"What makes you think you want to join our organization?"* These questions tell the interviewer that you are a confident person and are willing to answer questions that others may consider intimidating. *This is also a chance to slip in a question that you really want to be asked because you have an excellent response that can advance your candidacy.*

9.12 Some people feel that spending too much time in any one position shows a lack of initiative. What is your opinion?

The interviewer may be talking about you. Clarify the point at the beginning of your answer by saying, *"That might be a comment regarding my current job."* Then proceed with the response: *"But I do not think it applies because of the variety of challenges that I had to face and grew with—until very recently."* The point to make, if you can, is that it is not the amount of time in the position that is important but the diversity within the position itself. If this has not been the case, and you really have been stuck in a position for an extended period, highlight the changes and growth within the position.

> *Although technically I have been in the same position, I have been retained through four staff reductions that had a direct impact on my department. So even though the title changed, I have frequently had to work to determine how the job could be done in the light of change—and with fewer resources. We managed and thrived by constantly reinventing ourselves. So by title what appears to be the same was actually a position that had seen four major alterations with me in it. The positive side for me was the opportunity to grow in ways that I might not have considered had the downsizings not occurred.*

9.13 Have you ever had difficulty getting along with others?

If your answer presents you in a positive light, then give it as a strong answer.

> *As a matter of fact, yes. I was employed briefly by the U.S. Post Office at its main facility in Boston. I had problems from the start because I wanted to show how productive I could be. Every day, even though I was new, I was setting productivity records. The union steward and then a few of my fellow workers tried to dissuade me by letting me know in very direct language that I was disruptive and that my work habits needed to change or I would encounter difficulty in my work relationships. Even my supervisor felt the need to tell me to slow down. I had to leave.*

Of course, if you are seeking a position in another union environment, this might not be a good answer! If you do not have a strong answer, just state that you have always found a common ground to deal with others to accomplish the job at hand.

> *I realize when I start a new job that the current team may not buy into my arrival, but based on past experience, I am confident from day one that I will sooner or later become part of the team by not overwhelming*

people, but rather by looking for opportunities for me to contribute to their success as we grow together.

9.14 Have others ever had difficulty getting along with you?

There have been instances of differences in opinion or approach, some even passionate, but I have always tried not to get personal with these issues, and consequently, I feel that others have found me professional and effective. When we differed, we seemed to always find some common ground to proceed.

9.15 What are some of the things that bother/bothered you about your current/last job?

Always remember that you should never bad-mouth former employers or organizations; it sets a negative tone and raises questions about your potential loyalty. Preferably identify minor nuisances and inconveniences. Keep in mind that your interviewer is not asking for the purpose of correcting these problems. Preface your remarks with a comment that, *"For the most part I really liked my job but—as with any job—there were a few minor frustrations."* Then mention irritants that, if corrected, would have enabled you to be more effective.

One mail pickup a day.

There was an antiquated calendar used to track orders—a wipe-off board that you needed to leave your desk to check. I suggested using an online calendar so that everyone would be able to access it without losing time leaving their desks, but the department head was not responsive.

So many people never checked their e-mail.

People would hide behind e-mails rather than take the time to have face-to-face contact.

*9.16 What can I tell you about this organization?

If this question is asked toward (or at) the beginning of the meeting, it is poorly placed. You need to determine the interviewer's reason for raising it at such an early point. You need to be ready for it, though, because it happens.

You can let the interviewer know that you want to learn more about the organization's current operations (assuming that you have done research already and just need to be brought up to date).

Other questions that could meet this request include

Please share with me what, in your opinion, is the most unique thing about this organization that gives it its competitive advantage?

Who do you think will be your main competitors in the future?

If you are able to share this, tell me where the organization wants to be in three (five) years. What effect will that have on your unit? On this job?

An alternative is to say something like, *"I have no questions to ask at this time but will save them for later."* Remember that to say, *"I have no questions"* is perceived as a weak response because a real reason for interviewers to raise the question is to give you the opportunity to show how prepared you are for this meeting. They give you this shot to take the floor because they are not prepared to give you a lot of time and attention if your answer shows that you are not a strong candidate. If it does show this, they feel that their initial impressions have been confirmed and that the meeting should be ended as swiftly as possible.

When you are thinking about what to ask, do not panic. Here are some other suggestions. A great open-ended response that is perfectly appropriate here is either, *"How's business?"* or *"How is the company doing?"* Another tactic is to ask the interviewer, *"How long have you been here?"* Then follow up with *"How's business?"* If you have done your research, you can be more specific with questions regarding a new market, product, or location. Be certain of your facts before you open this door.

These can be winning responses because they get interviewers to talk about themselves. At the same time, the question implies that you are evaluating the interviewer and that, based on her responses, you will ask additional questions. So the conversation becomes an ever-so-slight test for the interviewer.

Refer to Chapter 12, "Now It Is Your Turn: Questions to Raise," and the "Organization Fact Sheet" you prepared in Chapter 3 (see page 50) listing the information that you need on the position and/or the organization.

9.17 What can you do for us (that someone else cannot)?

This is another version of "Why should we hire you?" You need to give a strong, brief answer. Discuss your skills ("can do") and your motivation ("will do"), relating them specifically to the organization and the position ("fit"). Combine those facts with a comment on your wish to be a part of this organization, and you have given a strong powerful answer. Think: "You need _____ and I can provide _____ because _____."

I feel that I have a unique skill set, combining technical knowledge, hands-on expertise, and an eye for design. For a photo editor, being able to visualize what the content needs to support its message is a valuable asset to the job.

*9.18 What do you know about our organization?

Aren't you glad you did research? Do not overwhelm. Sum up briefly the nature and scope of the organization, and make a brief comment on its age. *"I know that you have been a pioneer in the sewage treatment industry and have always led the way since your founding 23 years ago."*

9.19 What is the most difficult part of looking for a job for you?

Try this one out before the meeting. To appear effective, your comment might be something like, *"Getting my foot into the door of this organization."* Be alert for any comment that may seem to be whining, and do not turn this into a "you-asked-so-I-might-as-well-tell" session. Do not consider interviewers to be career counselors or therapists (even if they happen to be either). You are there to get a job.

9.20 What outside interests/activities occupy your time?

This question is included here because there are two aspects to it. One can be just small talk, trying to find out about you. The other aspect can be related to "fit."

If you are considering a job with a coin-collecting company, numismatics would certainly be a related interest. Do not mention too many outside interests because you may be perceived as having too many demands on your time already. Consider golf, tennis, and sailing. For example, mention golf if your research confirms that golf is a major corporate pastime, if business is generated through relationships developed during 18 holes of golf, and, above all, *if you already play reasonably well*. Do not under any circumstances pretend to be something that you are not because the stakes are not as high. A knowledgeable interviewer could expose you as a charlatan. Why take that risk?

Team sports are good if you participate and if it is a team environment; supporting local events as a volunteer is great for community-based companies. Highlighting your involvement with PETA is not so good if you are applying to a store selling fur coats! Be weary, too, of controversial organizations. If you enjoy target shooting, fine, but mentioning NRA certification for pistols takes the statement to a whole other level.

9.21 What question could I ask that would really intimidate you?

This is one of the most terrible questions to deal with because it puts applicants to a test that requires a most demanding answer. Once you state the question, the interviewer then asks the question that he would not have thought of asking you in the first place.

When you are preparing in advance for this question, consider all the questions that may come up so that this question from the interviewer is just an opportunity to answer another one. The only difference is that the burden is on you not only to provide a question, but also to be ready with an answer.

However, there is an alternative: choose a question that the interviewer has already asked. This accomplishes two things. First, your answer flatters the interviewer, who has already come up with what you consider to be a really intimidating question! Second, by identifying a question that the interviewer has already asked, you do not have to answer a tough question that the interviewer had not considered. You do not have to add to the arsenal. Again, you can also take the opportunity to slip in a question for which you have a strong answer.

9.22 What reservations do you have about working here?

If you have any, now is not the time to raise them. Quash the temptation to say something like, *"I only hope that I am good enough to make it here."* Instead, say: *"I see this position as a fine opportunity and the organization as one that I would be proud to be a member of. I don't have any reservations."*

9.23 What new insights do you feel you will bring to us from your experience in a different industry/position?

Unlike other questions that ask you to come up with justifications that show "been there, done that," this one seeks a response more like, "You need this, you do not have this; I can bring this."

> *I come from a small company where everyone had to be able to fill in for most positions in the department, regardless of their status. So as supervisor, I needed to understand all the jobs well enough to be able to perform them, if needed, as well as to hire replacements. That flexibility and willingness to do what is needed to get the job done will be an asset here at _____.*

9.24 Where does your boss think you are right now?

This is a nasty question to ask a currently employed applicant. Avoid being caught in a lie:

I arranged to take a vacation day/personal day.

I rearranged my lunch hour to make this appointment.

I came in early this morning to clear my desk and explained to my supervisor that I had a personal matter to attend to this afternoon.

As the entire department is being phased out over the next few months, we are all covering for each other as we go on job interviews; our department head supports this as long as the jobs are covered.

9.25 Why are you interested in coming to/working in/relocating to (city/ town)?

The tone of this question appears negative. Starting your answer with that comment may help to determine the interviewer's motivation for the question and her feelings toward the place. If you are serious about pursuing a top-level position at Wal-Mart, for example, you need to be very positive about Bentonville, Arkansas. You will not be forced to move there, but the firm does have staff meetings on Saturday mornings, and not only employees but their families are invited (and we would think expected) to attend.

Regardless of the location, *part of the job search process should include research on the location of the organization* where it seems most likely that you will be working. Keep your comments confined to the specific question. Suppose the location is not the most desirable, such as an inner city area that is ripe for urban renewal or a boring industrial park. Make the point that the reason for your interest in the location is the opportunities presented by the organization, which has chosen to set up shop there.

It is tempting to offer comments such as, *"I see that there is an excellent school system"* or *"Public transportation is a great selling point,"* but you may be disclosing information or topics that you may not want to open up for further discussion (that you do have children or plan to, or that you do not drive or own a car).

Observe whether the interviewer is failing to disclose a bias and is discriminating against you for whatever reason. You may want to add, *"Please tell me what made you ask that question."* This is an ideal way to get the interviewer to open up without your appearing unnecessarily aggressive.

If the distance appears to be a real trek for a daily commute, be prepared to answer this one and be sure that the job, if offered, will be worth the effort. *"I really love to work, so I am prepared to do what it takes for a job that I feel I will really love. As you can see from my résumé, I have in the past had ('almost as long' or 'even longer') commutes that were well worth the job I accepted."*

9.26   Why aren't you earning more at your age?

This is another terrible question from your point of view—"why" questions come across as judgmental, and when that is combined with intimating that you are not a financial success, it can be very uncomfortable. Do not succumb. Do not challenge the premise.

> *When I was just out of college, I considered other factors to be more important than pay. On-the-job training, exposure to experts in the field, and being associated with organizations that were breaking into new fields were forms of compensation that did not show up in a paycheck. I have been fortunate enough to be able to consider the entire package rather than just dollars and cents.*

If it is warranted, a mention of irregular and discretionary bonuses or great benefits (in addition to medical and dental, tuition refund, generous time off, or flexible work arrangements) might be included to demonstrate that any discussion of your past compensation must include other components to be sure that the discussion of the compensation package is complete and accurate.

*9.27   How much would it take to get you? What do you feel the position should pay?

The point in the interview process at which this issue is raised establishes the level of seriousness. If the question "How much would it take to get you?" is asked after three intensive interviews, it may mean that an offer is about to be negotiated. If, on the other hand, interviewers ask, "What do you feel this position should pay?" as part of the first interview, they may very well be trying to get applicants to knock themselves out of contention with the wrong answer or hoping that you will give a lowball figure that they can then use when you and others are extended an offer. Another reason may be that the interviewer has not determined the price and is using you to determine the amount.

If the question is raised early, such as anytime in the first interview, you may respond by saying, *"I really do not have enough details on the position in ques-*

tion to determine an amount." If the question is asked later, you cannot give such a weak response. If you are not clear about the duties and responsibilities of the position and how the position is pegged in the organization by then, you may be perceived as ineffectual and a poor listener to boot.

If you must answer, you can ask first about similar jobs (but not amounts at this point) in the organization. Try using a question such as, *"What other jobs in the organization are similar to this one?"* When you have been provided with this information, ask the salary range for those positions.

Continue by saying what you may feel is obvious: *"Are there any additional considerations that would require you to pay at a different level for this position?"* Notice that you are still trying to avoid mentioning a specific dollar amount.

If the answer is negative, then you may say that without additional information and without knowing the details of the benefits and other forms of compensation (bonus and incentive payments, last and next anticipated increase dates), it is difficult to provide a number worthy of consideration.

If you are still pressed, consider giving a range of numbers. An example is, *"Between $33,000 and $38,000 if the assumptions I am making about other factors are accurate."* Or, *"Based on the job as described, and without considering any other benefits, a salary of mid-five figures would seem appropriate."* Have some estimate in mind before you show up for the meeting; this should have been part of your initial research. If an amount was not mentioned in the specific job listing, perhaps there were similar jobs listed that did cite compensation levels.

Sometimes you get the interview without the benefit of any opportunity (e.g., job postings/want ads or recruiters) to determine the price for the position, or you have the interview, but you are not sure what position, if any, will be discussed. In such cases, try to find out at the first opportunity, without appearing mercenary. By asking, you negate any opportunity for the interviewer to ask the same question (unless she forgets that she told you, and if she did, doesn't your answer then make you seem astute?).

If the question is phrased "What do you feel this position should pay?" it is easier to deal with, but it is still stressful because salary is always a delicate topic. In this instance, you may defer if you do not have a reasonable understanding of the position's responsibilities and scope. You may comment on recent published salary surveys or articles in the trade journals, stating that information indicated a range for the job would be $_____.

Based on the information that you provided, and without knowing more, I will say that a salary of between $45,000 and $52,000 would seem fair from my knowledge of the marketplace and my understanding of what your competitors are willing to pay.

*9.28 Why do you want to work for us? Why do you want to work here?

This is a basic question that should have been running through your mind as you prepared for the interview and should still be doing so as you sit there talking. Of all the jobs and organizations out there, why are you here talking to us about this particular position? You may have talked about why the company should hire you—but why do you want to work for it? There should have been several good points that came up during your research or in the interview so far; now is the time when you need to share them.

However, this question, in either format, can be considered discriminatory if it is asked of minority candidates. The implication is that this is not the place for you to work. Regardless of your ethnic background, avoid sharing negative comments with interviewers, even if they speak disparagingly of the organization.

These are unusual times for organizations. With bitterness sometimes sweeping through organizations as they downsize, it is not that rare to run into line managers or human resources professionals who confide their bitterness. *Listen but do not participate, regardless of your feelings. You are witnessing a bizarre situation.* If you are subjected to a disgruntled employee's monologue during the recruitment and selection process, listen and keep your distance. You may win in two ways. First, a job offer may be coming your way because the person speaking to you liked you enough to open up without fear of retribution. Second, you are getting a deep insight into the organization from an insider—great data for you to consider when you are deciding whether you are in fact interested in joining the organization.

9.29 Are you surprised to be out looking for a job at your age?

How old do you look? How old does the interviewer think you are? Since there are legal protections from being discriminated against based on age, he cannot ask how old you are. Ignore the reference to age and respond professionally, moving the subject on to another.

All the employees were aware of the situation—I knew that my prior employer was talking about bankruptcy months ago. So I really was not surprised when it started looking to wind down operations. That was when I updated my résumé and jumped right in. It's great to see that companies such as yours are taking advantage of the decreased competition; your _____ product line seems uniquely placed for this economy.

---

*9.30 Your résumé suggests that you may be overqualified/underqualified/ too experienced for this position.

Why should I hire you? You do not seem to have the appropriate experience or education for this position. Interviewers may be letting you know that they have already written you off, and they may or may not be giving you one last shot at convincing them otherwise. This question cries out, "You had better show me or else!" Additionally, it may display the interviewer's true feeling, which is, "The clock is ticking, and I am running out of patience."

When this question is asked by a line manager who might even be your future supervisor, the question and your answer are even more important. You need to relate specific skills and experiences that qualify you. If the attitude is that you are overqualified, the interviewer may have monetary concerns. You are an attractive candidate, but she may be afraid that the firm will be unable to afford you.

Be delicate. You need to strike a balance between agreeing with the person's concerns on the surface and providing a convincing answer that neutralizes the concern expressed. One approach may be to start with, *"I certainly appreciate your comment, and I might agree with your concern.* [Try to avoid using *but* here.] *I wonder whether you have given attention to . . ."* Avoid using words like *enough* or *ample*, which may be considered a criticism and may put interviewers on the defensive because they may feel that they are being attacked. Once this statement has been delivered, a strong positive response must follow. The response should give interviewers the opportunity to easily agree that there is something in your experience that they did not recognize, while at the same time taking some responsibility for the interviewer's initially thinking otherwise.

> *I can understand your concern about my being "overqualified." That said, let me also share that even though I have moved up what might be considered two levels from the position we are discussing today, having been at that level, at this point in my career, the job as it has been described is a more attractive option for me. Frequent interactions with colleagues and peers are a more desirable challenge that I missed as I moved up the career ladder. Having had the opportunity to do both, I prefer at present the position we are discussing.*

> *I am not certain whether I stressed my experience in using both PCs and Macs, and I recently learned Dreamweaver. I have investigated and taught myself open-source programs to prepare newsletters.*

In a worst-case scenario, when interviewers are being kind and you know that you don't have any of the experience that they want, briefly and directly agree with the interviewer. Then move on to a positive statement that indicates your potential.

I have learned so much about _____ in the past few years that I have a fair understanding of my learning curve, so I feel very confident that I can be up to speed on _____ very quickly.

9.31   If you were going to Mars, what three things would you take?

Believe it or not, this type of seemingly nonsensical question comes up from time to time. One reason may be to challenge your creativity. Another is to determine how you act under pressure. Don't let the question floor you, even if it really bothers you. You cannot let the interviewer see that you are easily rattled. Start the answer with a disclaimer: *"I will give the question a shot, but please understand that I never took an astronomy course (or it was so long ago that I forgot most of it)."* Then give it a shot. A possible first choice is an expert in the field. A second choice could be sufficient oxygen to allow you to breathe in that environment, and a third could be enough fuel for the return trip.

Two out of the three items chosen show that you are serious about the basics, and the choice of the expert shows your ability to depend on others who are the experts so that it becomes a team effort. From a seemingly nonsensical question, an evaluation may have been extracted by the interviewer.

STRESS REDUCTION TECHNIQUES

❑ **Get off to a good start.** Get a good night's sleep the night before. Have a nutritious breakfast. Have travel directions and listen to news on traffic delays and weather information. Pack your "bag" ahead of time with business cards; copies of your résumé; the information you gathered on the company, the position, and the industry; and the list of questions that you want answered. Get there at least 15 minutes early, and know the name and location of the person you are meeting with.

❑ **Prepare ahead of time.** What are your weaknesses? What are your professional sore spots? Accept your lack of perfection and look for what you can do to compensate.

❑ **Avoid going on the defensive.** Some questions or situations (endless interruptions, a distracted interviewer, and a headache) are out of your control. Do not react—allow your prepared, confident side to take over.

❑ **Try taking the offensive** and turning the situation around. Answer a question with a question. *("Has this been a major problem?" "Have I said something to lead you to believe this?")*

❑ **Keep your cool.** Sweating, fidgeting, grimaces, and eye rolling send messages of acute discomfort (or worse), which may be interpreted by the interviewer as "has something to hide" or "cannot handle this interview—how can he handle the job?" Be aware of both your body language and the interviewer's.

❑ **Slow it down.** Don't blurt out an answer just to move on to another topic. Speak calmly.

❑ When in doubt as to what response to make, **take an unnoticeable deep breath, pause**, and try for as confident and sincere an answer as you can offer.

10

TAKING CONTROL OF THE INTERVIEW

The dynamics of interviewing can be exciting to the person who is sensitive to an interview's elements and has developed an appreciation for them. The person who understands the process is also more effective when serving as a participant. (This goes for interviewers as well as for interviewees.)

Whoever controls the interview has a leg up in the process as long as that person does not make the other person angry while doing it. Some say that the more job applicants can get interviewers to do the talking, the greater the likelihood that they will be successful. People love to hear themselves talk. So it follows that, if interviewers get to do a lot of talking, they will feel good about themselves. If they feel good about themselves, they credit the person who is responsible for this feeling.

Does control go to the person in the interview who is talking or to the one who is listening? The astute interviewer recognizes that the listener, with occasional intervention, gets to control the interview. An interviewer with little knowledge or experience of the process is more likely to consider the opposite to be true. A major way to control the interview is with questions. *The person who gets to ask the questions controls the interview—that is, until the other person starts to respond.* If the person who asked the question gives up control, then the person answering has gained control. It is up to questioners to determine whether the answer given was sufficient and then, in the spirit of the conversation, talk again. If they raise another question, they have again taken control of the interview. Like a tennis match, control can bounce back and forth between the players. One way this control is given is through the format of the questions (open-ended or closed-ended) and the type of answers elicited.

OPEN-ENDED QUESTIONS	CLOSED-ENDED QUESTIONS
Leave respondents open to answer however they wish.	Require a yes or no answer.
Respondents can take the answer in the direction they choose.	
Samples: "How was your trip in this morning?" "Why did you leave your last job?"	**Samples:** "Did you work over-time in your last job?" "Would you like a cup of coffee?"
Reason asked: to explore a topic.	**Reason asked:** to ascertain facts in a rapid-fire manner.
Purpose and intent: this approach works from the premise that rather than getting a yes or no answer, the interviewer is interested in using the question as an opportunity to get to know the applicant.	**Purpose and intent:** the interviewer is confident that there are right and wrong answers, so she prefers to ask questions in a quick sequence to find out if the applicant is answering appropriately.

We already discussed the topic of small talk, the period at the start of the interview that gives the interviewer the opportunity to set the mood. If this is done correctly, the tone that is set enhances what is to follow because it makes applicants more open to sharing their thoughts and concerns throughout the rest of the interview.

In this chapter, we consider two major categories of questions—open-ended and closed-ended—to consider how each type is used to maximize the effectiveness of the interview and how to deal with them.

The key to the effectiveness of the process is to be able to go back and forth with both open- and closed-ended questions to keep the conversation flowing with the information required to come to a conclusion regarding the applicant's candidacy.

Here is an example of a sequence of questions that an interviewer could use:

Question 1: *"Do you work overtime in your present job?"* Notice that this question requires the briefest of replies (either "Yes," "No," "Sometimes," or "It depends"). *"Yes."*

Question 2: *"What causes the overtime to occur?"* Now the open-ended question gives you the option of analyzing the reasons from your experience.

It is usually due to one of two factors—sometimes both. One is to cover when another employee is out because of illness or on vacation. The other is to respond to a surge in orders or a backup caused by weather or some external issue.

Question 3: *"On what basis are the workers chosen to work overtime?"* This is another open-ended question that allows you to elaborate.

Since we are a union/agency shop, we follow the collective bargaining agreement that is currently in place. It states that any opportunity to work overtime is to be offered strictly on a seniority basis.

Question 4: *"Did you mind working overtime?"* Getting specific with a closed-ended question leaves you no room to negotiate an answer. If you say that you hated it, the die is cast, depending on the organization's opinion of overtime. If you say something like, *"Frankly, sometimes it really bothered me"* (a long version of a "yes"), then take the opportunity to qualify your response. *"But, I have always been a team player, so if I am called upon, I will do what is asked of me, unless I have a prior obligation that I need to take care of."*

Question 5: *"Under what circumstances did it bother you?"* This is an effective interview technique: using closed-ended questions to focus and open-ended questions to explore the candidate's background.

Even though the organization's policy is that if you need to miss your shift, you have to call in at least two hours before the start of the shift, some employees don't check in until 15 minutes before the shift is to start. This is bothersome because some of us are asked to cover, changing our plans, and the supervisor needs to do extra work looking for staff members to stay longer.

So What Does This All Mean to You?

Control of the interview belongs to the one who controls the questions. The person providing the answers is following the lead of the questioner. If you consider an interview to be a dynamic situation, with control flowing from one person to the other, you will begin to get an idea of the importance of the question mix (open- and closed-ended questions being asked back and forth) as an opportunity to retain control of the interview.

Interviewers are required to obtain answers from your meeting that allow them to accurately determine the degree of "fit" between you and the organization, along with your level of expertise and motivation. The more the interviewer can get you to talk, the more likely she is to arrive at an accurate decision based on an effective interview process.

As the applicant, you also want information from the interview. First and foremost, you want to be offered a job. You become the interviewer when you try to extract information from the employment interviewers so that you can determine whether a job offer, if extended, will be acceptable to you. The more you learn about the organization, the more able you will be to make an informed decision.

For the sake of understanding the dynamics of the interview, therefore, the more you are sensitive to open- and closed-ended questions, the more insight you will gain into the effectiveness of interviewers and their competence. If interviewers ask only closed-ended questions, it may mean that they are in a hurry—or it may mean something else. The interviewers may be poor interviewers, or they may have no interest in you—and with this interview technique, being not too oblique in sending that message.

Note: You never want to upstage an interviewer. One way to avoid doing so is to attend to his interviewing style and performance level by meeting him at the competence level that he establishes. If the interviewer prefers closed-ended questions, you should not show any annoyance or frustration at not having the opportunity to really show what you know. Here an effective tactic may be to look for a question that sounds of interest to you and one that you feel will make you look good.

10.1   Do you have any plans for vacation this year?

No, we have not made any decisions yet, but let me mention plans that are in the works. Every three years, we all get together for a family reunion. This is the year for our next one. It usually takes place in late August and lasts for four days. The venue has not been finalized nor the dates. Would I have a problem getting the time off?

The interviewer might respond, "I am so glad you are telling me this now. Had you waited until after you started, your access to those dates would be dependent upon the requests of those with more seniority than yourself. Since you are letting me know now, if you are hired, we can see whether we can make that part of our offer and include it in your offer letter. What you need to do before we can make any decision is to get the specific dates.

The Easiest Type of Questions to Answer

The first point to remember is that closed-ended questions are usually the easiest to answer because they usually hint at the answer the interviewer is looking for, but, on the other hand, they do not allow you great latitude in giving anything but a narrow response that you might want to elaborate on. If the accurate response has a *but* attached to it, do be honest in your reply.

10.2   Do you work overtime?
Who needs further analysis before determining the correct answer? *"Of course I work overtime."*

10.3   How is your health?
Everyone is hale, hearty, and ready to serve.

10.4   We require people in this position to travel overnight frequently. How do you feel about this requirement?
"No problem." Or this might be an opportunity to ask for further details: *"I imagined that meeting with out-of-state clients would be a requirement; it makes a lot of sense to maintain the relationship. How often do clients expect a meeting?"* putting the emphasis on client needs rather than how much or how often you would have to travel.

10.5   Do you know how to use a SuperZippo PC and its major proprietary software package, Bogus Oats?
"Of course."

Or, *"Yes, I am using it right now with my current employer."*

Or, *"No, sorry, I have not had the opportunity, since we use the competing product _____ software. To determine how much time it will take me to get up to speed, please share with me what is expected of that software in this environment."*

Prepare for the Follow-Up

A good interviewer follows up with probing questions to see if your answers support your initial answer or to provide further information. After the Bogus Oats question, if you responded affirmatively, the interviewer could ask something to determine to what extent you are giving an honest answer.

10.6 Tell me what applications you use Bogus Oats for in your current organization.

Notice that the interviewer used the technical term *applications* to determine your level of PC literacy (or at least its jargon), and at the same time seeks to see what you are doing with Bogus Oats in your current situation. You cannot answer "yes" or "no," and even more probing may be in evidence if you have yet to agree that your familiarity comes from using Bogus Oats in your current organization.

The interviewer has raised a number of issues, and you are at liberty (and have the responsibility) to answer the question in the most appropriate way for you. Be honest when you are responding to closed-ended questions, or your bluff may be called. For example, the interviewer could say, *"I am so glad you are familiar with Bogus Oats! I kept getting an error message just before our meeting. Could you look at my screen?"* You thought it was a simple yes or no question, and now you are faced with taking the interviewer's PC on a test drive.

What if you have no knowledge of the software that is being discussed?

This position will require you to use Handy Dandy software on a daily basis. Are you familiar with it? Have you ever used it?

Three big don'ts to remember here—first, don't panic if you don't recognize the name. Second, don't fake it. Third, don't start your response with an apology.

"I am not familiar with this software but please share with me what you use it for so that I may consider the process I have been using to demonstrate to you how we accomplish this task at XYZ Company."

Consider the activity and see what you do to complete the task. You probably are either: using a similar product; proprietary software; or may still be doing the process manually. In any instance, you need to show that you understand the logic of the process—especially if it is performed manually. Speak professionally about the process and your understanding of it. Treat the software as a tool that will help accomplish the task and as something that can be trained. Whenever possible, you might even demonstrate that with your understanding of a different approach to the process that your alternative may even be better than theirs—and if that happens, you have put the interviewer on the defensive. If it does, however, be careful that you don't gloat.

Dry Runs

Identify several skills, experiences, or behaviors that you feel are essential to your candidacy. Then write a scenario with open- and closed-ended questions designed to elicit information from you. For example, if computer literacy is a key issue, the following exchange is likely to occur:

QUESTIONS ABOUT PC EXPERIENCE

What type of computer do you use at work?

"I use a desktop PC at work."

What software do you use on a regular basis to accomplish your tasks?

For each program you identify, state what output you generate with it. It will also be helpful for the interviewer to know what version you are using, as frequent updates are issued.

Are you responsible for designing reports, or only for generating reports that are designed by others?

What are your biggest problems with the software you are using?

Are there other software packages that would be more effective?

What are they, and in what way will they be more effective?

Do you have a PC/Mac at home?

What do you use it for?

Any topic involving your skills, experience, or work history is ripe for this type of conversation; you can envision follow-up questions to many of the answers you would provide to the questions posed in this book. There's no telling where the interviewer will go with her line of questioning. In the following exchange, notice the give and take and the information provided with each question.

Questions about a Team-Based Environment

10.7 Here at XYZ Corporation, we are a team-based organization. Have you ever worked in a team-based environment?

"Yes."

In what organization did you work in a team-based environment?

"In my current position at _____."

Please describe the way you work in detail.

"The Facilities Department is a team-based environment. There are seven of us, and we have a brief meeting at the start of our daily shift for two reasons: first, to discuss what occurred yesterday, and second, to make sure that we all know what we need to do today."

Is it a self-managed work team?

"It is."

How is the leader chosen?

"A key way in which we complete tasks is to have a person volunteer to take the leadership role for each project."

What is your role?

"I frequently volunteer for the leadership role and get it."

How frequently does the team meet?

"Daily, at approximately 8:15 a. m."

The questions can continue along various lines, such as discussing the projects that the team worked on, the composition of the members of the team, or how the work was reviewed—wherever the answers given might lead. Questions can end with your answer, or they can open the door to an entire chain of related questions, so to some extent, by virtue of the power of disclosure, you can control the interview and drive it toward areas that you want to discuss further (and perhaps away from those that you would rather not discuss). Your answers and the details that you provide can either open or close doors, and it is important that you consider where the questioning may take you.

QUESTIONS YOU PLAN TO ASK/ANSWERS YOU NEED

List five closed-ended questions that you would like to have answered in the interview.

1. _____

2. _____

3. _____

4. _____

5. _____

List five open-ended questions that you would like to have answered in the interview.

1. _____

2. _____

3. _____

4. _____

5. _____

GUIDE FOR OPEN- AND CLOSED-ENDED QUESTIONS

❑ **Practice** whenever you can. Develop a series of related questions on any topic by mixing open- and closed-ended questions to see the use of each type.

❑ Closed-ended questions **focus on a topic**; open-ended questions **dig deeper for content**.

❑ Try to **anticipate open-ended follow-up questions** when the conversation begins with innocuous closed-ended questions.

❑ What are the topics that **you want the interviewer to dig deeper into**? Keep those in mind so that you can seize any opportunity to open them up for further discussion if one of them is introduced.

❑ Look at the **questions that you want to ask**. How many of them are closed-ended to obtain focus, and how many are open-ended to get details? Recall that the purpose of the interview is for both parties to obtain information.

11

DON'T GO THERE!

QUESTIONS YOU MAY *NOT* WANT TO BE ASKED— BUT MAY HAVE TO ANSWER

For those of us living in the United States or Canada, government protection in the workplace stems primarily from common-law practices and traditions that go back to medieval England and to a primarily agricultural society.

The *employment at will* principle is a major common-law standard in this tradition. Briefly, it says that an offer to work (from an employer) and an agreement to provide services (by an employee) are based on a voluntary agreement (or contract) by both parties. Unless otherwise stated in writing by contractual wording, the agreement may be entered into for a good reason, a bad reason, or no reason at all, and may be terminated the same way. In this agreement, the principle tries to emphasize the fact that the agreement is between two independent parties and that the power of each is "equal."

However, as we know, employers have the upper hand more often than not because there are usually more applicants than there are jobs available. So the employer is permitted to hire and terminate for a good reason, a bad reason, or no reason at all, and, as already stated, this can be done without notice.

Traditionally, employers in this country have conducted the selection process in precisely that manner, and the federal government did not interfere until the 1930s, with the passage of the Fair Labor Standards Act (setting a minimum wage and overtime pay requirements) and the Social Security Act, followed by the enactment of civil rights legislation, commencing in the 1960s. Also in the 1930s, federal legislation was passed that protected the rights of workers who were union members or who had union sympathies, under certain circumstances.

The first law passed as part of civil rights legislation was the Equal Pay Act of 1963. This law protects women and men against gender-based pay decisions. In simple English, the law prohibits basing wage and salary decisions on whether the person being paid is a man or a woman. The primary beneficiaries were seen as being women because studies conducted at the time showed consistently that women were paid significantly lower rates than men for the same jobs.

The Civil Rights Act of 1964 was intended to protect the civil rights of all people; it prohibited discrimination based on the following characteristics: race, creed, color, national origin, and sex. Title VII of the Civil Rights Act of 1964 specifically prohibits discrimination based on those characteristics in any of the terms and conditions of employment (including, of course, hiring and firing). What effect, if any, did the Civil Rights Act of 1964 have on the common-law principle of employment at will? Employers are still entitled to make decisions regarding the terms and conditions of employment (including hiring decisions) for "a good reason, a bad reason, or no reason at all," as long as they do not violate the provisions of the Equal Pay Act, the Civil Rights Act of 1964, or any subsequent related legislation that expanded protection under the law to include the elderly, persons with disabilities, and Vietnam-era veterans, along with those who followed them.

Other federal laws that deal with private-sector workplace discrimination issues include

- Americans with Disabilities Act
- Vietnam Era Veterans' Readjustment Act
- Federal Pregnancy Act
- Age Discrimination in Employment Act
- At the state and local levels, protected categories sometimes include sexual orientation, same-sex partners, and nonsmokers.

What about Affirmative Action?

Affirmative action has been an important part of public policy since the 1960s. In 1966, President Lyndon B. Johnson created Executive Order 11246, which not only prohibits, under certain conditions, contractors of the federal government from discriminating against any applicants or employees in any terms and condition of employment with regard to race, color, creed, national origin, or sex, but also requires employers with 50 or more employees to take affirmative steps to correct past imbalances. There are two things to remember about this policy: first, this is not a law, it is an executive order, and second, organizations that are not federal contractors do not have to follow it. There are organizations, however, that are not federal contractors that have determined that affirmative action is good business policy. They have voluntarily adopted affirmative action steps to create a more diverse organization.

Affirmative action has been accused of introducing quotas into the workplace. Yet all the related guidelines and interpretations are supposed to be considered targets and guidelines. They are not to be rigidly adhered to or enforced to the extent that a quota is. To do so would be to go beyond what affirmative action is intended to do and to raise other discrimination issues (e.g., reverse discrimination).

When applying for a job, applicants should have current knowledge about the various employment laws if they are affected by them. Persons who have disabilities and are applying for jobs should know, for instance, that the Americans with Disabilities Act prohibits employers from discriminating against persons with disabilities and requires reasonable accommodations to be made, but it does not require any affirmative action steps to be taken.

Can Employers Still Discriminate? Yes, But . . .

A widely accepted misconception is that, because of the antidiscrimination laws, employers may no longer discriminate in the workplace. This is not true, as the selection process (as well as, in fact, the recruitment process) is by its nature discriminatory: some applicants are "discriminated out," and others are "discriminated in." The most discriminatory step of all occurs when the selection decision is made, because only one person is hired. All the rest are rejected. The decision to hire one person discriminates against all the other applicants.

What an employer may not do is discriminate against employees and applicants on the basis of any category that is protected by law. Employers may still ask irrelevant (to the applicant) questions as long as they do not touch on the categories that are defined and protected by this law. It is not just that employers may not make a hiring decision based on any of these categories; they would be inviting applicants to file complaints with the EEOC (Equal Employment Opportunity Commission) or their state human rights commission if questions pertaining to them are even raised!

For example, an employer who distrusts people who wear green socks may be prompted to ask, upon noticing that an applicant is not wearing green socks, "If you were employed here, would you wear green socks?" It is perfectly legal (absurd though it may be from a business perspective), under the common-law principle, to refuse to hire applicants who say that they would wear green socks, if the employer makes that a term and condition of employment.

There may be valid business reasons for what at first appear to be strange factors entering into hiring decisions. For example, if you are being considered for a job at a fragrance company and you go to the interview wearing a competitor's fragrance, the interviewer can reject you for your poor judgment in choosing a fragrance. This becomes more of an issue the higher you rise on the organization-al ladder. If you are interviewing for a vice president's position, the "mistake" (as interpreted by the interviewer) might be much more noticeable to the interview-ing organization than if you were applying for a position as an entry-level clerk.

You may think certain questions are illegal that are not. Users of tobacco products (smoked or smokeless) may be discriminated against, as may be persons who are extremely tall or short. Facial hair (or the lack of it) or visible tattoos may also be grounds for rejection, as can be rings (e.g., ear, tongue, or facial), whistle-blowing, and filing for bankruptcy.

WHAT IS AN ILLEGAL QUESTION?

The most obvious illegal questions are those that directly address characteristics of the person that are protected by law and that are not required to be answered for a determination of the person's eligibility.

11.1   Where were you born?

This is a very obvious example of a blatantly illegal question. More subtle but just as illegal is another form: "That is an interesting accent. Where are you from?" Title VII of the Civil Rights Act of 1964 prohibits discrimination on the basis of national origin. If interviewers ask these questions, they have an agenda. If the purpose of the meeting is to consider an applicant for the job, then the answer will influence, if not determine, the interviewer's conclusion.

Other patently illegal questions are

What religion do you practice?

I see that we live in the same community. I've never seen you at temple. Where do you go?

Under certain unusual circumstances, such questions may be considered appropriate. See the following discussion of bona fide occupational qualifications (BFOQs).

An Exception to Remember—BFOQs

BFOQs are bona fide occupational qualifications. An otherwise illegal line of inquiry may be construed as legal under certain specific circumstances. State and local laws concerning them may be more stringent than federal laws. Local laws, for instance, may have a sexual orientation prohibition as well. So consider the community in which the employer is located. These laws specifically permit discrimination by a specific organization if the unique need of the job requires it. For instance

- If the employer is in the catalog business and needs a model for children's, men's, or women's clothes, the employer may legally consider the gender and/ or age of the applicants and include the requirement in advertisements.
- A church, synagogue, or mosque has the right to insist that persons hired to fulfill the religious aspects of any open position (e.g., priest, minister, imam, or rabbi) be practicing members of the same religion.

Difference between Illegal and Inappropriate Questions

11.2   Are you married? Are you single? Divorced?

This question is in a gray area. On the face of it, *it may not be illegal to ask the question, as long as you ask it of both men and women applicants and there is no state or local law that protects applicants from discrimination based on marital status.*

On the other hand, this is a terrible question because it may raise legal issues, and once a complaint is filed, the burden of proof rests with the employer. Interviewers may be extremely objective and careful to conduct highly structured interviews, but the complaining applicant probably doesn't know that. The key is to remember that all questions raised during the job interview should be job-related. If a question isn't job-related, then it is best to not ask it. It is difficult to imagine a job that would *require* that a person be single, married, or divorced.

11.3   Do you have any children? Do you plan to have children? Who cares for your children while you work?

Again, although such questions may not be patently illegal and may be asked *if they are asked of all applicants* (male and female, married and unmarried), they should not be asked. Consider what the purpose of the question is. It is certainly one that may cause annoyed applicants to file complaints because they do not know (even if the interviewer says so) that the practice is to ask every applicant the question. Who needs a complaint filed?

Managers seem to want to raise this question because they feel that any commitment that includes children makes the person less reliable. The question is more frequently asked of women than of men, since research indicates that in the United States, in approximately 95 percent of those situations involving one or more children who are under the age of five, the primary care of the children is the responsibility of a woman. In addition, women are also the primary caregivers for the elderly and disabled. Rather than considering that individuals with greater responsibilities would have a greater commitment to being employed, some employers have a preconception that such individuals would have higher absentee rates and less of a commitment to their careers.

If you are asking this question because you would like to learn more about my commitment to my career, let me assure you that the time I have spent building my career and the drive that I have to work will not be replaced with domestic issues.

If you are asking because you are concerned about coverage, I have very reliable primary and secondary child-care coverage. I assure you that I will not be distracted from my work because of child-care issues. When you discuss my performance with my references, you will learn that even overnight travel is never a problem.

Why Do Employer Representatives Ask Illegal Questions?

- *They may be ignorant of the laws.* The person asking may have little or no interviewing experience and no training on the legal aspects of the interviewing process. Alternatively, the interviewer may be a foreign national who is on assignment here from an organization with headquarters overseas. In other countries (and even in international agencies located in the United States), questions that are forbidden here are part of the process. Questions regarding age, marital status, and family are taken for granted and are a demonstration of the organization's interest in the whole person.
- *They may ask these questions out of arrogance.* Certain strange people try to raise illegal issues. For odd reasons, they feel the need to test their authority. They are going to ask anything they "damn well please," and no human resources professional, or, for that matter, anyone else, is going to stop them. To make their point, persons with this attitude take any recruitment and selection opportunity to ask illegal and other inappropriate questions, whether for their shock value or because they wish to intimidate, and anyone who is looking for a job needs to be prepared for them and their questions. It begs the question why you would wish to work for an organization that would allow this type of behavior.
- *They may ask these questions out of innocence.* Those who have had little or no training frequently are poor interviewers and may just go off track and forget that some subjects are not open for discussion. They may even have the

training and/or experience, but they do not have the proficiency required to interview effectively. The problem may also stem from the mere fact that they had no or little time to prepare for the interview. Whatever the reason, these persons frequently try to impress themselves with the ease with which they are able to ask questions. They do not realize that the key to effective interviewing is not thinking about the next question, but rather concentrating on the answers. As a result, when these persons realize that they have run out of questions but feel that they are not ready to close the meeting, they blurt out an illegal question ("Are you looking forward to going home to a home-cooked dinner?") or a high-risk one ("Do you have any children?"). These interviewers may be intimidated by the applicant and be seeking to find common ground (children of the same ages, similar religions) in an effort to make *themselves* more at ease. Or these questions may be asked by line personnel who have not been adequately briefed or are not sufficiently experienced with appropriate interviewing practices.

What to Say When You Are Asked an Illegal or Inappropriate Question

First of all, you may consider answering the question and getting on with the interview if you feel that the information is neutral to your candidacy. You may also consider not answering the question by stating, *"That really is a question that I prefer not to answer. Can we move on to another topic?"*

What about the worst-case scenario? What if the interviewer persists with illegal or inappropriate questions? If an interviewer asks you such a question, always remember the first and most important rule: *do not take it personally.* This is not to say that you should excuse it or treat it lightly. The point is that, if the question is being asked of you, it has probably been asked of who knows how many others. These interviewers are continuing to ask illegal questions because they have *not* been confronted with a refusal to answer. They may have a number of reasons for pursuing this line of inquiry, as discussed in this chapter. If they continue to ask what you perceive to be one or more illegal or inappropriate questions, you may attempt to address the issue firmly but diplomatically by repeating your response. If they still continue, their message is one of either total ignorance of the law or complete disregard for it. It is to be hoped that you will never have to face this type of encounter. If you do, no matter how desperate you are for a job, remember that it is more than likely that the job offer will never come anyway. So our suggestion is that you terminate the interview and decide whether to file a complaint.

Gender Bias Questions

Unfortunately, there continues to be bias in the workplace, and those who are asked tainted or illegal questions are usually women or members of other perceived minorities.

11.4   What is your maiden name?

This is really about your marital status, and it is obviously asked only of women applicants. The legal way to ask the question is to ask on the application (not in the interview), "Have you ever used any other names? If so, give them and briefly describe the circumstances." If the question is asked outright in the interview, counter with, *"I assume that you are seeking this answer because you are going to perform a reference check. My entire professional life has been under my current name."*

11.5   This job requires long hours. Will this be a problem for your spouse and/or your children?

I have had an excellent attendance record and have been available for time-consuming projects, such as _____, which was completed on time and within budget.

My job is an important part of my life. My family realizes and appreciates that fact and is very flexible with my schedule. When you check my references [if this is so], you will see that my record and my credibility attest to that standard of performance.

11.6   Where does your spouse work?

The answer to this question allows interviewers to learn whether you are married. Other insights may be gleaned from your answer without asking. If your spouse does not work, interviewers know that you are the sole support of your family and that there may be children or other dependents to inquire about. If your spouse is working, interviewers have an opportunity to peg your status by both where your spouse works and what your spouse does. (This is a follow-up question or one that might not even need to be asked if the applicant wishes to disclose the information.) In addition, if interviewers learn that your spouse works, then a follow-up question could be who takes care of the kids if they need care during scheduled work hours.

This is a particularly interesting and important line of inquiry if the applicant is interviewing for a job that requires any overnight travel. When they are not direct, interviewers can get into trouble with illegal questions. With the increasing numbers of single parents and two-career families, organizations are—and should be—rightfully concerned about outside commitments and coverage. To stay in legal territory, however, they should mention their concern to all applicants—male and female—to get the answers they need.

Certain stereotypes and misconceptions of minorities may underlie questions regarding marital status, number of children, and employment of spouses. Similar brief professional answers are the best response.

11.7 Whom should we notify in case of emergency?

This question still sometimes appears on application forms. *It is inappropriate to ask the question before the person has been hired.* It may be asked just because "it has always been there" or because interviewers are probing for information that they may not otherwise be able to obtain. They are hoping that you will name your spouse. Not only do interviewers learn that you are married without having to ask, but they also get a workplace telephone number for your spouse, thereby discovering what he does for a living or whether he works at all. If the question appears on the application form, you may leave it blank. Most people reviewing your application do not even notice. If it comes up, say, *"I didn't bring a workplace number with me, but I will get it for you."* Don't mention the workplace number of whom by name or relationship. Chances are that this will be the end of the inquiry. If it isn't, ask the reason for the persistence now, and apologize one more time for the information not being available. Then leave it at that.

This inquiry can be a ruse to determine whether the applicant is gay or not by seeing whether a male or female applicant gives the name of a contact with a different last name but the same gender.

11.8 If you were offered this job and you accepted it, you would be required to work with a mostly male (and/or Hispanic, or born-again Christian, or any other identifiable group) staff. Would this be a potential problem for you?

This question is asked generally of women who are applying for a job in a traditionally male area, but it may also be asked of men in an area that is traditionally occupied by women.

No, in my profession, I am expected to deal with a lot of men [women]. I have experience dealing with a variety of people. I have always managed to build credibility, and I pride myself for creating a positive working environment for every member of the team.

None at all. The key to an effective working environment is to establish performance standards and then make sure that each person on the team understands them. Each team member should realize that he or she will be evaluated based on adherence to those standards. To be effective, the team needs to universally accept these basics regardless of their backgrounds or experience. Once this is communicated, then each member of the team knows what is expected and has a team to do it with. This becomes a major benchmark for growing the team because it is more important than perceived differences.

The question may be a practical one, however, and a reasonable addition to your response is to question what language the group uses to communicate during the workday: *"Please tell me what language is used throughout the day to address workplace issues."* If a language other than English is used, a practical concern for you is how you will deal with this issue if you are offered the job but not fluent in the prevalent language.

National Origin Questions

11.9   That is an interesting accent. What country are you from? What country are your parents from? You have an unusual last name. Where were you born?

Other variations may include

> *What is your native language?*
>
> *What language do you speak at home?*
>
> *I see on your résumé that you mention that you are fluent in _____ .*
>
> *How did you have the opportunity to learn that language?*
>
> *Are you from China or Korea [or Africa or the Caribbean]?*
>
> *You are a citizen of what country?*

Interviewers may raise such questions either because they have run out of questions or because they are truly curious. You may wait for them to make an additional comment to indicate how the question is job-related (e.g., if you are being considered for an overseas post). You may certainly ask, *"Are you concerned that my birthplace has some bearing on how I will perform if you hire me?"* Or you can say something to engage and redirect the interviewer by talking about someplace you might have visited for a time. The most direct response is to let the interviewer know that you have a problem with the question. Go on to say that you wonder whether the question indicates a negative judgment on the interviewer's part and therefore might eliminate you from further consideration and terminate the interview.

These inquiries are by their very nature against the law unless there are specific BFOQ reasons for asking them. Interviewers from the departments where the job openings exist when representing employers may be careless and are frequently poorly prepared for the interviews. BFOQs are becoming more and more rare. Fluency in the German language may be a BFOQ requirement for a German bank doing business in Chicago, but German citizenship or birth is not.

11.10 What do your parents do?

This question is raised by interviewers who are interested in determining whether the applicant comes from a home background that is in some way related to the work habits that this organization thinks it requires. Even though this is certainly an interesting question for a biographer, it is not job-related. Would it be a positive or a negative to be from a prominent family whose founders had created an empire or a dynasty? Should it be held against (or in favor of) the applicant if this is so? To make the point more obvious, consider the following: more and more Americans are going to jail. To make matters worse, in some communities, it is a status symbol for a family member to be in jail. If that fact were to come out during a discussion of this question, how would the interviewer respond?

How do you answer this question? *Do not share more information than you are required to, and try not to share your annoyance.* You have no idea where these questions are coming from—a former employee may have taken a lot of sick leave to take care of an ill parent, or the interviewer may have a soft spot for those with single parents. For example, if your mother was a widow:

My father worked hard his whole life, but he passed away years ago [if this is true]. Is there something else you seek on this subject that I could help you with?

State briefly what occupation your father had. If you don't know what your parent did, don't mention it. Say instead that your parents separated at an early age and your father, your mother, or some other relative raised you. However, if a parent had a positive tie-in with the organization or industry where you are seeking employment, you may want to mention this fact.

My mother is a marketing analyst, and she has always pointed out to me your innovative advertising campaigns.

*My father ran a gym and took me to wrestling matches starting when I
was five years old. I recognized quite of few of the Superstars featured
in the photos in your lobby.*

11.11 Do you think you will have a problem working in a department that is predominantly white (or black, or Asian, or another ethnic group)?

On the face of it, this is not an illegal question. Yet it has undertones of bias and
is a question that may be asked of anyone who is different from the predominant
ethnicity, race, or national origin of the work group. As we mentioned earlier, the
question is intended to determine whether applicants will fit into the work group.
Look into your background for examples to cite your effectiveness with diverse
work groups.

*I am confident that I will be an effective member of the work team. In
the past, I have had experience working with _____, and my record
shows my effectiveness at performing successfully in that environment.
For example, at XYZ Organization, the work team was composed of
_____ and we increased production by [some statistic] while I was
there. Let me ask, though, what language do the group members speak
while performing their work tasks throughout the day?*

Questions Suggesting Religious Bias

11.12 Are you a religious person? What denomination?

This question is never appropriate, with a single exception. For those seeking
a position as a religious professional—priests, nuns, rabbis, imams, ministers,
or teachers in a religious school (although for the latter, the grounds are legally
shaky), where belief is still considered a BFOQ—the question may be asked.
Even if you are seeking a job that has no religious aspects at all in a religious-
affiliated institution, your beliefs (or disbeliefs) may not be the subject of inquiry
during the application process. For instance, you do not need to be a practicing
Roman Catholic to work in the accounting department of the Archdiocese of
New York.

11.13 Will you have to take time off for any religious holidays? Can you work late on Fridays? Can you come in on Saturdays or Sundays for special projects? We sometimes work overtime on weekends. Will this be a problem for you?

For what reason is the subject being raised? Have you chosen to disclose your
religious beliefs on the application or on any other documentation? Is it because
of your attire? Is the interviewer's assumption accurate? Regardless of its basis,

the phrasing of the question is still not appropriate. If the interviewer has a concern, then the organization must provide specifics of what may be required in the department you are applying for. If there is no conflict with the duties and hours, say so.

If there is a conflict or the potential for future conflicts, you should determine the nature and degree of the possible conflicts in advance. If there are one or two days (or one or two weeks) a year that you absolutely need to have off, say so. However, do so in a way that demonstrates that you will be willing to do whatever you reasonably can to accommodate the employer's requirements and workload (even though the guidelines and court decisions say that the burden is on the employer to make reasonable accommodations). By your suggesting ways to do it (e.g., using vacation entitlement), you show employers that you are looking to work with them to find a solution. Do not choose to place the burden on employers by saying, in so many words, *"The law says you must accommodate me, so don't bug me, or I will take you to court."* Instead, say

> *If there is not enough time during the workweek to complete the tasks assigned, I will certainly work with you, as my supervisor, to complete the task however I can. If that requires weekend work, if I am unable to work on a particular Sunday or Saturday, I have no problem with working the other day.*

Interestingly, with diverse lifestyles becoming more mainstream, the reasons that persons are against weekend work of any kind may have nothing to do with illegal topics. If weekend work is something that an organization requires, you should hope that the question is raised so that you can make a job decision with one more issue in front of you while you are going through the process. The answer to question 11.6 may be an appropriate response to this line of inquiry as well.

11.14 I noticed that you did not shake my hand when I offered it. Is there a religious reason why you chose not to do so?

If the answer is yes, answer this question in a matter-of-fact way. *"Yes, the only reason is religious. I certainly intended no ill will."* If there is another reason (e.g., you do not like to touch other people because they all carry germs), say so briefly and succinctly, if you wish. But don't show yourself to be a fanatic over the issue.

We have a colleague who recently retired as the head of employment for one of the most prestigious health-care institutions in New York City. One of her major responsibilities was the recruitment and selection of candidates for positions at all levels throughout the organization. Throughout her career, she refused to shake anyone's hand in either personal or professional situations. She would merely say that she feels strongly that germs should not be shared through handshakes, and she hoped the other person understood that there was nothing personal intended.

11.15 What organizations do you belong to?

Regardless of the intent of the inquirer (the term *inquisitor* almost seems appropriate), remember that you are the one who is giving information. Disclose only what you wish to. If you want to show your professional expertise, give an organization or two that are particularly appropriate for your profession. Be careful not to fudge here or on your résumé. Also, make sure that you have the completely accurate current organizational name. There is nothing more embarrassing than to identify yourself as a member of XYZ Organization, only to learn that the name was changed to ABCD four years ago.

Avoid disclosing information on membership in controversial organizations—unless you want to. The National Rifle Association comes to mind. Environmental groups, the Communist Party, and pro- and anti-abortion organizations are others that may distract the interviewer from staying focused on the task at hand—namely, trying to determine whether to screen you in or out as a candidate for employment.

Age Bias Questions

11.16 How old are you? Oh, I did not expect you to be so old/young.

Age continues to be a sensitive area, so avoid any references that may inadvertently trigger a response from the interviewer. *"You may not be old enough to remember when . . . "* is a comment that you should not make, as it will shift the interviewer's focus to age sensitivity when prior to that she had not been focused on age at all. *"They don't do things the way I am used to any more"* is another comment that magnifies age differences. Your physical appearance, too, may trigger age concerns. No applicant—male or female—should ever be dressed in a way that might be considered frumpy or dowdy. How should you look? Contemporary and professional. How can you be sure? Stay connected with those in the workplace to see what appropriate attire is. You should look slightly better than those who already work there—at the very least, look as if you were an employee.

If the interviewer, for whatever reason, asks, *"How old are you, anyway?"* consider this an opportunity to take the offensive, but do not gloat. You could be humorous or nasty:

Old enough to know that I want to work here.

Young enough to enjoy every day.

Give the answer and wait for the next question or, if you feel that you do not want to disclose your age, withhold that information. A third alternative is, *"I prefer not to say,"* or, looking puzzled, *"What makes you ask?"*

At the same time, if the possibility of your being offered a job will be destroyed if you admit to being the age that you are, we suggest that you fight for yourself and deal with the person who is acting against the law. Since she has no right to ask the question, you are not obliged to answer. This situation seems similar to one that an HR head shared with us when he hired an administrative assistant. When her references were checked, the administrative assistant admitted that she had lied when she applied for the administrative assistant job: she did not include the fact that she had a law degree. When confronted, she said she knew that if she had included the law degree, she would have been deemed overqualified and not hired. The HR VP allowed her to stay, and to our knowledge she is still there.

Whichever approach you choose to take, after you give your answer, be absolutely quiet and wait for the interviewer to say something. Do not break the silence, regardless of how long it lasts. The longer it takes for the interviewer to say anything after your answer, the more of an advantage you have.

11.17 Can you read well enough to take this test? A more polite version of the same question may be, Are you prepared to take the test today?
This question deserves a quizzical look as a practical nonverbal response. If you are not able to give one effectively (or to camouflage your anger with a poker face), swallow your desire to retort, *"Now what do you mean by that?"* Be non-plussed and state in very even tones instead, *"I am sure I can,"* or, *"Yes, I have my contacts in."*

11.18 Change drives this organization. How flexible are you? How do you deal with change?
This may be a nonbiased question that is asked of everyone in a dynamic, constantly changing environment. It may also be reserved for those who seem to be

too old to be flexible or competent. One of the most biased folk sayings in this country is the terrible one about not being able to teach an old dog new tricks. Be brief, direct, and focused with your answer.

I am very accustomed to change. My last position certainly is an indication of how I thrive in a changing environment. Let me give you a brief example . . .

11.19 Don't you think you are a little young to be seeking this position?
This is an obvious age bias question that discriminates against youth.

If you are looking only at my birth date, I might consider the comment appropriate, but if you look at my résumé, you will see that I worked throughout college in this industry as a(n) _____. Since that was when our technology was in its infancy, I have literally grown up with the industry.

11.20 Would you be willing to start at a lower salary level because of your inexperience?
There may be a hidden agenda here because younger hires, women, and minorities frequently are paid less for a position than men. Think ahead about your answer to this one. *Ask what the range for the position is.* Recognize that a premium is to be paid for those who show more expertise, and one way to do that is through demonstrated experience. If the organization has wage and salary ranges, interviewers may or may not share that information with you. Even if they do not, you show your sophistication by asking the question.

I appreciate that salary may be commensurate with experience and that I may command less. That is acceptable as long as the salary is within the range for the position. I am very interested in working for your organization, and I am confident that my performance will merit salary increases according to the organization's policy.

11.21 What kind of discharge did you receive from the military?
This question was probably carried over from previous versions of the employment application and really should not to be asked. If it appears on the application and you prefer to leave it blank, do so. If there is a problem and you feel better addressing this issue in preparation for your job search, contact the Veterans Administration prior to your job search to determine whether there has been any change in the status of your discharge. If there has not been, can anything be done to change that status so that it looks better whenever an employer asks the question?

Questions Addressing the Disabled

11.22 Are you disabled? Are you handicapped? How did you become disabled? How long have you been disabled? How severe is your disability?

These sweeping questions are not directly job-related and are not permissible under the guidelines established by the Americans with Disabilities Act. Interviewers may specifically ask about a disability that might prevent you from performing the specific job for which you are applying without some accommodation, but they may not pose the question in any of these broad strokes. If you have a disability that is not readily apparent, in order to be protected by the law, you must indicate that you are disabled. (Isn't that a catch-22 for disclosure?)

The questions about the circumstances under which you became disabled and/or the length of time that you have been disabled are not related directly to job performance. These issues are history and therefore may prejudice the interviewer. There was, for example, a quadriplegic who had suffered a spinal cord injury that left him disabled from the waist down. The injury was the result of a gunshot wound in a gun battle that raged around him while he was an innocent bystander. Because it was a gunshot wound, however, unfair assumptions were made about his lifestyle and his morals, and he suffered discrimination while seeking employment. One reason for sharing this story is to be careful when the topic of a disability arises. In this case, the applicant obviously shared too much information, possibly in the hope of generating sympathy; had he said, "I was in an accident," no assumptions would have been made.

The law requires that job descriptions break down tasks into two categories: essential and nonessential. The *nonessential tasks* are those that a disabled person would not be required to perform if she were unable to do so. The *essential tasks* of the job are those that must be performed. The Americans with Disabilities Act requires that for essential tasks, a disabled applicant be considered for the job, even if reasonable accommodations need to be made.

One last comment on this category: the term *handicapped* is currently considered derogatory, and the term *disabled* is the more accepted term. The reason is the history behind the word: it goes back to the 1600–1700s and began with a lottery game known as *Hand in Cap* in the 1600s, which involved players placing money in a cap. Later on, in horse racing, extra weights were given to the strongest horse to even the field.

Other Illegal or Inappropriate Questions

11.23 Have you ever filed a workers' compensation claim?

A *workers' compensation claim* is a request for payment to be made to an employee as a result of an injury or illness caused by work. (If the injury or illness is not work-related, if time off is required, then it may be considered a disability.) There is sometimes a belief that workers' compensation claims are filed by malingerers. This is why the question may be of interest to employers.

It is against the Workers' Compensation Laws to withhold a job from an applicant because of prior workers' compensation claims. To ask the question is on its face completely illegal, and there is no excuse for asking it. You can confront the interviewer and say that the question is illegal. You can say, *"I do not have to answer that question."* The interviewer may not be pleased with the exchange and will probably also assume that you have had claims or else you would not make an issue of the question. Looking puzzled and surprised, you can honestly ask, *"Why am I being asked? I am able to carry out the job requirements as I understand them."*

11.24 Have you ever been a target (or victim) of sexual harassment? Have you ever filed a sexual harassment (or any other EEO or human rights) complaint? Have you ever been involved in a sexual harassment claim as a witness?

These questions are raised to determine your proclivity to take legal action in the workplace. The primary issue is whether employers have the right to ask such questions.

They do not. However, our opinion is that because they do, you should be careful with your answer. To say that you have filed suits raises questions about whether employers will face the same problems with you as an employee. Whether or not justice was on your side, discussing the problem only raises doubt and uncertainty in the minds of most interviewers—regardless of whether they possess the same EEO-protected characteristics as the applicant.

11.25 Has a sexual harassment complaint ever been filed against you? Have you ever been found guilty of sexual harassment?

This is a tough one because, once the question is raised, you need to answer honestly. Be careful from the point of view of self-incrimination. However, if there was an investigation and no cause was found, take the view that the complaint was without merit. Because the complaint was ultimately withdrawn, give an answer based on its ultimate determination and not its initiation. On the other hand, if the question is raised and you were found guilty of sexual harassment, admit it and state the circumstances. Mention that the consequences you had to deal with were serious enough to ensure that you will never be accused again (if that is the way you truly feel). To deny the situation is to promote an application with an obvious lie that can be verified. If and when the truth is uncovered, termination and humiliation could follow. Some employers accept the fact of a complaint if the applicant is honest and up-front about it. The alternative is to create a false impression and take the risk that sooner or later the word (and rumors) will spread—even if the case did not make it to the media.

Whistle-Blowing

If your employer is engaged in what you perceive to be illegal or unethical practices, and you call a government agency or some other organization (e.g., the newspapers or an environmental group) to alert it to these practices, you may end up without a job. Frequently, there is nothing illegal about such a termination— or, to put it another way, in the private sector, the whistle-blower has no job protection. If you are meeting with an employer who has a great and squeaky-clean reputation, you may find a receptive ear for what you were trying to accomplish with your last employer. You may disclose what happened in response to a question if you choose to do so. Prior to the meeting, you should determine whether, if the opportunity presents itself, you will disclose what happened. If you decide that you want to disclose it, then rehearse what you say before the meeting so that you are certain that the way you present it is the way you want it presented. Even then, we would encourage you to pause to consider the pluses and minuses of disclosure. You are taking a real risk. Is it worth it?

> *When I was at _____ organization, one day one of my clerks brought an item to my attention that to her seemed odd. A vice chairman of the corporation had presented her with a few gift cards from our employer that are usually awarded to low-level employees to purchase glasses for his personal use. She wanted to know what she should do. I could have said, "Just accept them," but I knew that she and her colleagues were interested in what I would do. I called the regional manager. He said that he would have to call me back. When he did, he said that auditors were on the way, but that we should accept the cards and give the officer his glasses. It turns out that this fellow had stolen more than $500,000 from the company in this way, and I felt that I had done the right thing. Interestingly, no one in management ever thanked me, and I definitely got the impression from that time on that management would not mind if I left.*

11.26 Have you ever been arrested?

This question is not to be asked. In this country, a person who is arrested is considered innocent until proven guilty. If there is any line of inquiry that the employer should pursue, it is to discover whether the applicant has ever been convicted of a crime. If the arrest question is asked, usually on an application form, and you have not been convicted, I would answer the question as if the word *convicted* appeared instead. It really is a breach of trust and illegal to probe into a person's arrest record and not pay attention to whether that person was convicted or not.

11.27 My kids are always sick with colds and flu. How about yours?

This is an interesting way to ask a question with an innuendo. First, if the question is the first to address the issue of children and dependents, it may also be a subtle way to determine whether you have any. Second, the question may be raised to learn whether you will be absent from work frequently. Third, the question may be used to anticipate whether your presence in the organization will translate into high utilization of the organization's medical plan.

If you have no kids, say so and be quiet. If you have kids and you feel that you can honestly say it, mention that you have been fortunate, as your kids have always been healthy. Add that you have always been prepared, however, for sickness and injury coverage because you realize the importance of planning and preparedness in that area. If you have someone either nearby or living with you who would be the primary care provider, mention it. Your answer is stronger (and demonstrates your professional approach to your personal commitments) if you mention this person, but including it is not necessary.

Do not under any circumstances disclose too much in terms of a list of recent illnesses or injuries, even if you feel that it is a light topic because now all the crises have passed. You are lingering on the topic and probably coming across as verbose. You may be perceived as someone who has been burdened with a difficult family situation.

11.28 We have a great medical plan. Did you get stuck with a lot of bills last year?

It doesn't take a rocket scientist to determine the interviewer's probable reason for asking this question. Even if that was not the interviewer's intent, now is not the time to find out. There is no reason for you to disclose your personal situation. So don't do it, regardless of how much you are tempted. For the most honest, let me add that, even if last year was the worst ever, the medical costs can always be higher. So even in this situation, you certainly may honestly say no. What may be "a lot" to one family may be nothing to another (and vice versa!).

DEALING WITH ILLEGAL/INAPPROPRIATE QUESTIONS

❑ Interviewers **should not ask them,** and **you do not have to answer.**

❑ In all circumstances, **you can control the amount of disclosure** when you are faced with an illegal or inappropriate question. If the truth of the matter can help your candidacy, consider offering the information at an appropriate time.

❑ Interviewers or organizations that insist on asking illegal questions or that have **a bias based on sex, race, color, national origin, religion, or disability (or perceived disability) may be doing you a favor** by revealing their true colors early in the interview process.

❑ Even though it is disappointing and frustrating to be asked illegal and/ or inappropriate questions, **do not allow your professionalism to slip.**

❑ **These questions are illegal whether they are asked orally or on an application form if they are asked before you are offered the job.** However, questions as to your social security number, health, age, gender, and marital status may be appropriate after you are hired for insurance reasons and EEO reports.

❑ In the worst of cases, to follow up and **make a claim of discrimination** against an organization that asks illegal questions, contact your local federal Equal Employment Opportunity office.

12

NOW IT IS YOUR TURN

QUESTIONS TO RAISE

"**D**o you have any questions for me?" is one more question that you really should expect. Since an interview is a conversation with a purpose, not a monologue, applicants, as participants in the conversation, may be required—or actually expected—to ask questions also. Of course, the applicant could always respond, *"No, thanks for asking. I have no questions at this time, since our discussion up to this point has really been comprehensive."* If the applicant does not ask questions when she is requested to do so, she may be viewed as having "failed" her part of the interview because the interviewer may feel that the applicant

- Is not sufficiently interested to raise questions.
- Is too shy, reserved, or unassertive to take the risk associated with asking a question.
- Does not have enough information or experience to raise questions.
- Feels that the interviewer has done a poor job, as he has not sparked any curiosity, raised any issues, or elicited any participation during the course of the discussion.

Questions that applicants are expected to ask during the interview must not be considered unimportant. In effect, applicants who don't ask questions can provide the right answers to all the questions posed to them, but still leave interviewers in doubt as to their level of interest. This is not to say that you must ask a question—any question—in order to "pass." On the contrary, if the give and take during the interview was ideal, all (or at least most) of your questions should have been asked and answered at some time during the process. In fact, if the interview has been an effective one, questions may readily pass from the interviewer to the applicant and then back again throughout the interview. However, even in this ideal situation, the applicant should be ready with at least one question when she is asked, "Do you have any questions for me?"

Before the Interview

Before the meeting, while you are doing your research, the more you learn about the organization, the more questions you will probably have about how the organization operates, what it is looking for in a new hire, and the specifics of the position that remain unanswered. Getting ready for any employment interview should include the preparation of questions that you need answered in order to decide whether to proceed or whether to accept an offer. There are some questions that you need to have answered early in the interview process in order to be able to discuss your candidacy intelligently.

The questions that you wish to have answered start out with the one original question: "What is the purpose of this interview?" Is it to be offered a job? If the end of your first interview is quickly approaching and you still are not sure, you need to ask, *"Do you have a specific job in mind?"* If the response is yes, then your thought process needs to determine what information you need in order to agree to continue with the process and to help you ultimately to make a decision if the job is offered to you.

Do not forget, too, that the organization, if it really takes its role seriously, should play an active role in selling itself to you during the interview process. If you are too concerned with *giving information* and for whatever reason did not pay much attention to the *getting information* aspects of the process, you may find yourself seriously deficient when it comes to deciding whether you want the job if it is offered because you lack many details that would be really helpful in making your decision.

During the Interview

You should write down your questions before the meeting. But what do you do with that sheet of paper during the interview? Show it or not? What about reading your questions from a sheet of paper and taking notes during the interview? We suggest that you keep that written list to yourself, since it may prove to be a distraction or may indicate to the interviewer that you are not sufficiently organized to remember what you want to know.

Currently, in our society, it is not considered appropriate to take notes during an employment interview. Our society is so litigious that tape recorders and note taking in any other form (such as paper and pencil) are considered threats—not to mention the difficulty of juggling a notepad, papers, or a tablet. That said, how do you remember the answers to the questions you raised? You should debrief yourself immediately after each and every interview (refer to the "Interview Follow-Up Worksheet", pages 206–207). The primary reason is that we all forget more than 60 percent of anything that we have been told within three days after hearing it. The sooner after the meeting that you review the answers, the better the chance you have of retaining the correct answers.

Pitfalls and Risks

Does raising certain questions put you at risk? When you ask questions, you are still providing "answers" and information to the interviewer. So, yes, there can be a risk. The burden is on you to determine what questions to ask, how to ask them, and, most important, when to ask them. Keep in mind that the best answers are those given to the questions that are *not* asked. Every question that you do not have to ask is one less to be worried about asking.

"Thanks for sharing your business model. I must admit, however, that I am unable to determine how you make a profit. Would you please share that information with me?" This comment, when made at an interview for a senior HR job with a dot-com company, brought the interview to a swift end with a big thud. The applicant later also disclosed that the question made the interviewer so angry that, as the redness rose in the interviewer's face, the applicant worried that he was about to have a heart attack. He didn't, but the applicant did notice that seven months later, the company had shut down. A sensitive nerve had definitely been touched in the interview.

In addition to asking an inappropriate question, there is always the risk that the question is a good one, but its timing is off. For example, if you ask, "What benefits are offered to employees here at XYZ Organization?" during the first few moments of your first interview, you will probably never need to know the answer. The interviewer is most likely to consider you to be more interested in the benefits than in the job or the organization (unless, of course, you are interviewing for a position as a benefits manager in the human resources department).

On the other hand, if this question is asked at the very end of the recruitment process, the moment is appropriate. The issue should be discussed before the offer is made so that the applicant has the opportunity to obtain this information to help her in making a decision about joining the organization. If you feel comfortable waiting for an offer to be made before asking the question about benefits, then wait. Remember, the best questions are the ones that are not asked. The organization, in its own interest, may share this information without your asking.

What can go wrong with asking questions? If you were not paying complete attention, you might forget that the information had already been given—and you have now given away your lack of attention or memory skills. Not being up to date on current events regarding the organization and asking about a product or division that has recently been discontinued *and* whose discontinuance was covered in the industry press lets the interviewer know that you did not do your homework. Be careful to avoid continuing to ask questions and ignoring signals that the interview is over, such as noticing that the interviewer is repeatedly looking at his watch or blatantly thanking you for coming. "Why?" questions can come across as judgmental (that goes both ways).

Consider asking the following questions as you go through the interview process, not only to demonstrate your professional bearing, but also to get the answers you need in order to determine whether the organization and the position under consideration are worth pursuing.

Questions to Ask Recruiters, Headhunters, and Employment Agencies

Meetings with recruiters and agencies are "screening interviews." If the interviewers are satisfied that you are a possible "fit," they will refer you to the organization directly for an interview. The organization (the client) is given either a copy of your résumé or a synopsis of your experience and qualifications prepared by the screener. If the representative indicates that she wants to "present" you as a candidate, this is a great opportunity for you to do your own "screening interview" to decide whether you wish to proceed.

If there is no outside firm involved in recruiting candidates to fill a position, these questions may still be asked of the HR recruiter, who usually performs the initial screening interview internally. The first three questions and the last in the following section would not be appropriate, but the others would be.

Is this a retainer or a contingency assignment?

How long has the client been with you?

How long have you had the assignment?

May I have a written job description?

To whom does the position report?

Why is the position open?

How long has the position been open?

What does the position pay?

Are there other types of pay, compensation, or perquisites that I should take into consideration?

Who will be interviewing me?

What is this person's position/title/management style?

Who will make the final hiring decision?

Are there any other written materials that I can review before I agree to a meeting?

Do you have any other similar open positions with other clients?

Questions that You Need to Have Answered in Order to Make a Decision

These questions assume that the information being asked for is not a matter of public record or available to be researched. These topics should be introduced with a brief statement, such as, *"Prior to this meeting, I tried to research _____, but I was not able to find much information."* You may learn that it is a new company or that it had a recent name change or has been acquired (although those last two alternatives should have been available through online searches).

Is the organization privately held? If yes, who owns it?

How long has the organization been in existence?

What is the mission of the organization? Does it currently have a strategic plan? Would you share that plan with me?

How many employees do you have?

Where are your other locations?

What are the organization's current major challenges?

Have there been any layoffs?

When was the last one?

Are more forthcoming?

May I have a copy of the current organization chart, employee hand-book, in-house publications, and job description?

Was this job posted internally?

Are you also looking within the organization to fill the position?

Have you published your earnings report for last year/last quarter?

Do you expect your recent rate of income/sales increase/decline to con-tinue this year?

Do you feel that I have the characteristics necessary to be hired and to advance in this organization?

How firm are the organization's requirements for the position?

What do you feel are the most important aspects of this position?

Who will be interviewing me? What is this person's position/title/man-agement style?

When will you have to make a hiring decision?

Who will make the final hiring decision?

How soon do you want to have an employee in place?

How long have you worked here?

What do you like about this organization?

Would this position lead to other job openings?

Can I visit the department where I would be assigned or get a tour of the facility?

How would you describe the culture of the organization?

Are there other ways of meeting the requirements of the position that may enhance the value of my experience/strengths?

Would you be able to share any financial information with me? Sales? Net income?

Does the _____ department create its own budget, or is one established for it by the corporate group?

How does the organization regard its employees?

How many applicants have applied for this job?

How long do you think it will take for you to make a decision?

What could I say or do to convince you to offer me this job?

Can I telephone you in ____ days to inquire about your decision?

and

Follow-up questions on any topics brought up in the course of the interview that you would like more information on, particularly if that information would affect your potential position or department. These may be the most important questions to ask, as they show that you are attentive, interested, and able to discern what the organization's possible priorities are.

When you were talking about your Web site and the addition of on-line ordering, I wanted to know how that was working out. I have seen the impact of electronic orders on sales, and I wondered if your projections were being met.

Can you tell me more about your new central fulfillment center? Has the cost savings been what you expected? I saw coverage of its opening and hiring of staff in the local news.

RAISING YOUR QUESTIONS

☐ Make a list of information that **you need to know** about the organiza-tion and the position in order to make an informed decision if the position is offered to you. Include information that you need in order to discuss the position intelligently; however, do not include infor-mation that might have been readily available if you had done basic research. Going down that road will only label you "unprepared" or "not interested."

☐ Establish a **priority list** for your questions. Certainly, details about the position itself would be number one on the list, as most job postings do not include much more than the basics. Logically, how the posi-tion relates to the organization's performance (is it a cost or a profit center?), the overall financial health of the organization, and plans for the future would all affect job security in the near term.

☐ **Review the list before your interview**, along with any information that you have gathered, so that everything is fresh in your mind (particu-larly if you have more than one interview scheduled that day).

☐ **Take your cues from the interviewer** and follow the topics introduced. When discussing the organization's management, for example, do not bring up questions about the position's location at headquarters.

☐ **Interviewers want to hear intelligent, well-thought-out questions** that show that you are interested in your own future and job security as well as in how your contributions will add value to your prospective employer.

☐ **Frame your questions for your audience.** General questions are best for the HR department to answer. Specific details about the position and day-to-day operations are ideal for the manager. Strategy ques-tions are best delayed until you meet with senior management.

13

WHEW! NOW WHAT?

You have thanked the interviewer for his time and for all the information he has given you. You have asked and gotten answers to most of your questions. You have exchanged business cards, and you are now out on the street, in your car, or in a taxi. With the completion of the meeting, your work is not done, however. Answers are not sufficient. You need to analyze the answers, review what worked and what did not on your end, and answer the questions that were hovering in your mind the whole time: *Do I think I got the job? Will the company call me back? If someone does call, do I really want this job? And am I willing to take the salary offered, or do I wish to negotiate more?*

Right after the interview, debrief yourself using the "Interview Follow-Up Worksheet" (see below). If you are asked back for a second meeting, this will enable you to recall the details of today's meeting. When you telephone to determine whether the position has been filled (by the date the interviewer indicated), you can ask any follow-up questions about your interview or candidacy, such as

---

INTERVIEW FOLLOW-UP WORKSHEET

Organization: _____

Interviewed with: _____ Date: _____

Title: _____ Location: _____

How did you get this interview? _____

Was this the first interview? _____ Follow-up? _____

Setting of interview: _____

Approximately how long did it last? _____

Did it start on time? _____

Purpose of interview: _____

Position interviewed for: _____

Salary range: _____

Overall impressions of the organization:_____
_____

Overall impressions of the position: _____
_____

Grade yourself: what did you do right or wrong?_____
_____

Grade the interviewer: What did he or she do right or wrong? _____
_____

What would you do differently? _____
_____

Are you still interested in the job? _____
Why? _____
_____

Do you think the company is interested in you? _____
Why? _____
_____

When will the position be filled? _____
How will the company/you follow up?_____
Comments: _____
Sent thank you e-mail/letter on _____
Were you offered the position? _____
If yes, are you accepting it or negotiating further? _____
_____

Details:
If it was not offered, did the company state why not? _____
_____

Would the company consider you for similar/other positions? _____
_____

Would you consider another position with that company? _____
Comments: _____
_____
_____
_____
_____
_____

Was there anything specific in my interview or background that you felt was lacking?

If any other comparable positions open in the near future, would you be in a position to contact me?

Surprisingly, a large percentage of candidates miss out on the professionally courteous step of sending a thank you letter (either snail-mailed or sent via e-mail, whichever is the method you have been using to correspond with the organization). This essential follow-up serves many purposes:

- *It shows that you have good manners* and that you recognize the time and effort that the interviewer put into the interview.
- *It recaps the meeting* to show that you did pay attention; interviewers appreciate feedback too.
- *It reminds the interviewer* (and anyone else you met with) of your specific qualifications for the position.
- *It allows you to ask for the job* (again).
- *It states what the agreed-upon follow-up will be.*

See the "Sample Thank You Letter" (see page 209). There are three sections to a polished thank you letter (or e-mail, if you prefer). (There is no certainty that your letter arrived unless you hear from the person to whom the letter was addressed, which is why a telephone follow-up after the thank you letter is recommended.) The first section literally says "Thanks" and refers to specifics from the interview: a tour of the facility, a topic that was discussed, or introductions to others. This is great feedback for the interviewer. Refer again to your "Interview Follow-Up Worksheet" (see pages 206–207) for any salient points of the interview that you can refer to specifically in the letter that would help the interviewer remember you and show that *you* remember the interview. The second portion is the "sales" section, reminding the reader of why you are an excellent candidate for the position and following up on any open items from the interview. The "closing," also important, confirms what the agreed-upon follow-up will be. Do not forget to ask for the job!

SAMPLE THANK YOU LETTER

(This should be written on your letterhead or sent using a professional e-mail address.)

Ms. Helen Trent
Human Resources Manager
H. G. Lippincott Manufacturing, Inc.
123 Main Street
Euclid, Ohio 44123

Dear Ms. Trent,

Thank you for spending time yesterday to interview me for the position of Senior Engineer—Waste Management Division. I knew that H. G. Lippincott Manufacturing, Inc., was a pioneer in sewage treatment development, but I was excited to hear about all the other environmental areas in which you are also currently involved.

As promised, here is a copy of *Garbage* magazine that contains my article "The Myth of Recycling." I feel that my areas of interest and expertise are a perfect mesh for the direction of your organization for the next decade, particularly with your recent successful bid to take over the recycling plant for Cleveland. Having dealt with expansion at my prior position in Indiana, I am confident that I can add value immediately.

I look forward to hearing from you soon and I am excited at the possibility of working for H. G. Lippincott Manufacturing, Inc., a recognized environmental leader. If you have additional questions, please contact me by telephone or e-mail.

I will telephone you on _____ to discuss the next step since I am convinced that the position we have been discussing would be a perfect match. I am hopeful that you feel the same.

Sincerely,

Ms. Jean Marie Jones

Enclosure

Sizing up Your Prospects

Whatever time you have spent finding, skimming through, deciding to buy, purchasing, and reading this book has been an investment in yourself that will help you to achieve your goal of finding the job you really want and one that you can be successful in.

Whether you chose to read this book from cover to cover (presumably you aren't expecting a surprise ending) or, as we recommended at the start, to select the most beneficial sections first, this book has provided valuable insights into job searching through the question-and-answer process of the interview itself.

The insights gained are also effective in your communication exchanges, both professionally and personally. Communication is one of life's experiences that grows in appreciation, enjoyment, challenges, and excitement as you devote more attention and consideration to its various elements and nuances. The "art" of conversation has fallen on hard times as a result of, first, its lack of use and then, because of lack of attention (and practice), its misuse. What is most difficult to fathom is that the need to communicate is increasing dramatically at the same time that our communication skills are in a precipitous free fall. It is really one of life's great ironies that our educational system, the proliferation of TV and the Internet, and the general acceptance of a lower level of ability to communicate (exacerbated by the challenges created by political diversity, multilingualism, and texting) are forces to be reckoned with at the same time the workplace is desperate for improved communication.

Sexual harassment, religious practices, disabilities, the increased inflow of non-English-speaking immigrants, telecommuting, teleconferencing, texting, smart phones, e-mail, the Internet, the global marketplace, and even voice mail all require increased communication skills. Technology only adds to the importance of saying the right thing, at the right time, and in the right way. PCs that don't work, software that doesn't function, lost cell phone signals, baffling technological manuals—all of these demand greater communication efficiency and effectiveness.

Q and A

The greatest tools for starting, continuing, and ending a conversation are questions and answers. The questioner has the opportunity to direct the conversation. The astuteness of the answerer, in more subtle ways, determines the extent of control to be given to the questioner. During the employment interview process, the more job applicants realize this important fact, the more effective they are.

The best questions are the ones that are not asked. If interviewers can get applicants to talk about topics and issues that are perhaps awkward or least desirable, they are more likely to obtain more complete and open answers. Unaware applicants (who are perhaps not wise enough to read this book) may open up and "tell all" to persistent interviewers, blurting out opinions and information that they had never planned to give (or even thought about before being asked for them in the interview). Effective interviewers can lower applicants' defenses by providing an environment that makes them want to share their entire lives—the good, the bad, and you know whatever else!

The "New Way" to Find a Job

With good jobs decreasing and competition increasing, those who are successful in landing a job interview will be the ones who have an edge. Getting leads and finding opportunities are essential ingredients, but once you find them, the job is still not yours. Unlike a treasure hunt, in which the map leads you directly to the treasure, the job search is loaded with steps and traps along the way. As long as interviewing continues to be the selection test of choice for most organizations in every sector of the economy, those who interview best will get the jobs, even though they may not necessarily be the best in other areas. Candidates must recognize that the best "products" do not always sell; a lot depends on the ad campaign, product placement in the store, and the buyer's mood. Understanding this will help applicants see that, even if they are the best candidates, they will not get the offer if they are poor interviewees. Once you identify an opportunity, preparation for the interview becomes crucial to your success. Failing to prepare is taking an unnecessary gamble and squandering an opportunity.

If we can expect to change careers at least three times in the course of our professional lives—not to mention the many different jobs we may have—then learning the skills needed to land the job that we want and developing them on an ongoing basis become increasingly important. How many interviews will we need to make those three or more career changes? How many will we "pass" by getting the job offer?

This book has made the argument that being prepared for the job search offers a number of other benefits, including

- *Improved communication skills.* Being able to carry out your end of an effective interview makes you more adept at the communication process—an increasingly demanding and valued skill.
- *Greater professional bearing and confidence.* If you master the interviewing process, you will grow in confidence with the increase in your communica-

tion and conversational skills, a primary requirement for moving up the career ladder.

- *Heightened personal awareness.* The better you listen to yourself and others, the more adept you will become at understanding yourself, your strengths, and your weaknesses. Once you recognize these, the better able you will be to work on self-improvement.
- *Increased energy.* Instead of worrying about the next question, you find yourself thrilled to have a chance to respond.
- *Recognition of the art and science of interviewing as a constant learning experience.*
- *One more opportunity to grow and have fun with the work that you do.*

If, as you go through the book and your interviewing process, you feel that your résumé needs improving (there is no such animal as a "one-size fits all job openings" résumé), or your entire job search seems stalled, with few callbacks for interviews, may we suggest our other publications to get yourself reorganized and reenergized:

More Answers to the 201 Most Frequently Asked Interview Questions
Get a Job in 90 Days or Less
Get a Job in 30 Days or Less
24 Hours to the Perfect Interview
Wow! Résumés for Creative Careers

If you seek assistance in the negotiation phase of the job search process, consider our title, *Perfect Phrases for Negotiating Salary and Job Offers*, to get you through the most important last steps.

INDEX

ABOUT THE AUTHORS

Matthew J. DeLuca, SPHR, is a senior consultant with the Management Resource Group, Inc.—a human resources consulting firm, in business for more than twenty years, providing a variety of practical people-driven organizational solutions. Matt is also the coauthor of several books including: *24 Hours to the Perfect Interview, Get a Job in 30 Days or Less,* and *Perfect Phrases for Negotiating Salary and Job Offers*. He teaches HR and management topics in corporate settings as well as at the graduate and undergraduate levels of the Zicklin School of Business at Baruch College (City University of New York) and the Polytechnic Institute of New York University.

Nanette DeLuca is a principal with the Management Resource Group, Inc., and coauthor of *24 Hours to the Perfect Interview, Get a Job in 30 Days or Less,* and *Perfect Phrases for Negotiating Salary and Job Offers*.